NEW HOME SALES

THE BASICS
AND
THE MAGIC

Suzanne Neff
and
Richard Tiller

© 2009
Suzanne Neff
www.SuzanneNeff.com
813-541-7816

Richard Tiller
www.RichardTiller.com
703-283-3902

All rights reserved.

Printed in the U.S.A. by Tiller Marketing Services
P.O. Box 531
Herndon, VA 20172-0531

ISBN 978-0-9630722-2-1

Table Of Contents

Chapter 1 Turning Basics into Magic......................................5

Chapter 2 The Mental Side of Selling 21

Chapter 3 Getting the Sale Started..41

Chapter 4 Showing Your Homes and Sites 67

Chapter 5 Handling Objections 95

Chapter 6 Closing 123

CHAPTER 1

TURNING BASICS INTO MAGIC

If you want to achieve success in new home sales, you will need to learn the basics. If you want to achieve greatness, you will also need to learn the magic. This book will teach you both.

Mastering the basics means learning, practicing and perfecting the right skills and processes, and we will show you how to do this for each stage of the sale. But what about the magic? Can the magic of new home sales be learned and perfected the way skills can? Yes, absolutely. After all, even magicians learn their craft, practice it, and continue to improve. In new home sales the skills and the magic – the science and the art – go hand in hand. Each enhances the other.

Of course, the magic of new home sales does not deal in the supernatural or the occult. It does not involve illusion or trickery. We are talking about magic in the sense of something that is wonderful, fascinating, extraordinary, and hard to explain.

What is the magic of new home sales, and where does it come from? This chapter will give you an overview of what the magic is all about. Then the rest of the book will show you how to use the magic to bring the basics to life – enhancing your skills with your own unique power.

How do you learn the magic of new home sales? There's no mystery to this magic, and you don't need a wand or a chant to bring it to life. The magic of new home sales is already built into you, and it's easy to find. If you focus on the following ten priorities, the magic will simply come to you. When you add these priorities to the basics that we will study throughout this book, you will reach the highest level of success in our wonderful profession.

Make Sure You Have the Passion

Great salespeople love to sell. If you ask a variety of new home salespeople why they chose this profession, you will get a variety of answers. "I love homes." "I love people." "I love to help people improve their lives." "I love to solve problems." "I love the home building industry." All of these answers reveal virtues that will make you a better salesperson. But a great salesperson will add one more: "I love to *sell* homes."

Greatness in our profession comes more easily if you believe that selling homes is fun, no matter what market conditions surround you. Even when selling is hard, it's still fun. It produces a unique joy and satisfaction that nothing else can replace.

The magic of selling relies partly on a passionate spirit. Great salespeople protect this spirit. They keep nourishing it with positive thoughts, refreshing energy sources, and a vital sense of purpose. No matter how much they accomplish, they want to keep learning and improving. If the passionate spirit goes, so does the magic. Do you have a passion for selling homes? If you're not sure how to measure your passion, then try this question: *How good a salesperson do you truly want to be?* Guard your spirit carefully. Keep nurturing your desire to improve, and your passion will take care of itself.

Connect With Your Customers

Connecting with customers goes beyond skill and technique. The magic of selling grows when you are sincerely interested in customers – in who they are, what they want, what they say, what makes them tick. This kind of interest enables you to connect with customers in a way that builds trust, and trust lies at the heart of any successful relationship.

Your interest in your customers is not only in them as people, but also in where they are trying to go, and how you can help them get there. **The most important connection you can establish with your customers is the connection of** *shared purpose.* Of all the salespeople they have met, you are the one who will help them get where they are trying to go. This is a huge element in the magic of new home sales, and it will remain a primary theme throughout this book. **A sense of shared purpose is the strongest kind of rapport you can build.**

Be the Salesperson They Are Looking For

While the basics of selling are about skill, the magic is about personality, temperament and demeanor. It comes from the heart. Customers want to see five things in a salesperson in order to experience the salesperson's magic.

1. **Confidence.** Your confidence becomes their confidence. It provides the encouragement and reassurance that are so important in life-changing decisions.

2. **Enthusiasm.** Your enthusiasm also increases their confidence. Enthusiasm is engaging. It makes people want to hear more.

3. **Joy.** Customers want to buy from happy salespeople. Joy is another source of reassurance for customers. Make sure every customer sees that you love what you do, not only because you enjoy it but also because you believe in it.

4. **Relaxation.** We think, feel and act more confidently and effectively when we are in a relaxed state. In fact, relaxation is the highest state of performance. Just as you are at your best when you feel relaxed, your customers will also be at their best when they are relaxed, so project your relaxed state to them. They will be more decisive if they are experiencing the magic of confidence, enthusiasm, joy and relaxation.

5. **Purpose.** We said that your strongest connection with customers is a sense of shared purpose. Great salespeople are purposeful by nature. As with confidence, enthusiasm, joy and relaxation, purposefulness can be contagious, too. However

confused, unmotivated or ambivalent a customer may be when they first walk into your sales office, they mustered up enough purpose to be there, and that's a start. Your purpose is to join forces with them to get them where they want to go.

Ideally, you will develop the kind of relationships with your customers where they won't want to buy a home from anyone but you. These five characteristics that customers most want to see in a salesperson provide a strong foundation for your relationships with them. They are also characteristics that will enable you to have the greatest impact. Of course, other characteristics are important as well: friendliness, kindness, honesty, a good sense of humor, and many more. But the magic of selling is inspired more by confidence, enthusiasm, joy, relaxation and purpose, so make sure they are part of the experience you provide. They set the stage for the next element in the magic of new home sales.

Seek To Achieve Resolution

Just as great salespeople are purposeful by nature, they are constantly driven to achieve resolution. A resolution-oriented temperament is another source of magic in selling. You feel a vital sense of purpose and urgency to resolve things. Your passion for resolution is so strong that failure to resolve a situation is not an option.

By connecting with your customers on the level of shared purpose, you have already engaged them in a way that other salespeople cannot. Now your shared purpose guides the sale from one resolution to the next. You gain momentum as you move from one stage of the sale to the next by resolving a series of decisions. This is when the magic of selling comes into full bloom.

As you might expect, the most resolution-oriented salespeople tend to be the strongest closers. Resolution is what closing is all about. Strong closers do not need to have aggressive personalities. They do not view closing as a conquest, but as a decision-making process that begins early in their relationship with a customer. One decision leads to the next. Smaller decisions lead to larger ones. Decisions make or break the sale. Without decisions there are no sales.

The willingness to make decisions is also the truest buying signal a customer can give you, even more than enthusiasm. Enthusiasm can be a buying signal, but it can also be simply a personality trait. Some people are simply enthusiastic by nature. But if they cannot make decisions, their enthusiasm is of no value.

Assume the Leadership Role

Another way to add magic to your selling style is by taking the leadership role in your relationships with your customers. Customers want your leadership.

As your relationship with each customer develops, there is usually a leader and a follower. Regrettably, many salespeople choose the role of follower. They feel more comfortable handing the position of leadership over to their customers. You will hear them say things like, "I don't want my customers to think of me as a salesperson. I want them to think of me as an assistant buyer." Or they might say, "I don't want to sell a home to a buyer. I want them to sell themselves." Another example would be, "Today's buyers are more sophisticated. They know what they want. If they want my home, my job is to help them get it."

To be fair, these salespeople have good intentions. They want their buyers to be happy. They don't want to push anyone into buying a home that isn't right for them. They believe their job is to provide good service and do the right thing. This is correct thinking for new home sales. We have a serious responsibility to our customers, and we need to embrace this responsibility unselfishly. However, there is one more piece to this puzzle, and it is a huge piece. Our responsibility to our customers also includes leadership. They expect this from us.

Customers know we are salespeople. They just don't know if we're any good at it. They expect us to try to sell them a home, and serious customers are surprised if we don't. When you are confident in your role as the seller, it makes your customers more confident in their role as buyers. Showing confidence in your role as leader and seller is often just what the customer needs in order to feel as though they have finally found the right place and the right salesperson. That is the kind of magic that brings the sale to life.

Sell To Customers As Though They Will Buy

Speaking of confidence, you will sell with a lot more confidence and a lot more magic if you sell as though your customer is going to buy. Think of all the times a rookie walks into a tough selling situation and gets instant results. We call it "beginner's luck." But what is beginner's luck in new home sales?

When you first begin selling homes, you get excited every time a customer comes in. They're coming in because they want to buy a home! All you need to do is help them realize why they should choose yours, and how happy they will be once they do. After you grow more experienced, you may grow less excited about visitors. After all, most of them probably won't buy from you anyway. If you sell one in ten you're doing well in many markets.

You started out selling to everyone as though they were going to buy. But if you're not careful, you could slip into the habit of selling as though they are not going to buy. Many potential sales are left on the table that way. Self-fulfilling prophecy is a huge factor in selling. Whether you believe your customers will or will not buy can have an enormous effect on the way you sell and on the level of success you achieve. When you interact with customers as though they will buy, you become more energized, enthusiastic, confident, purposeful, interested in your buyers, and involved with them. Your customers in turn feel more involved, and even more empowered, by your contagious energy and confidence.

There is only one thing you can be sure about your customers at the beginning of your relationship, before you get to know them. **They came to you, you didn't go to them. Assume they will buy until they prove to you they won't.**

Make Customers Feel Wanted

Customers are like everyone else – they want to feel wanted. Part of the magic of selling occurs when your customers feel that you want their business more than anyone else does. It's not that you need it more. You are not desperate. You simply want to sell them a home more than your competition does. How do they know this? Because you care more about them; you're more attentive; you're more interested in them, more curious about them. You enjoy them more. You want to help them get where they want to go. You want to understand them, but you also want them to understand you – your company, your community, and your homes. You want them to understand why other people choose your homes. Throughout the later chapters of this book we will discuss a selling style that engages customers more deeply at your community than at other places they visit by making them feel wanted without feeling pressured. Making customers feel that they are wanted more at your community than any place else helps your community to "feel right."

Don't Stop the Sale

Momentum is one of the main ingredients in the magic of selling. Throughout the selling process, your goal is to keep the sale moving from one stage to the next, resolving issues and decisions along the way. Each time you meet a customer, you want to generate momentum as quickly as possible, and then keep that momentum going as long as possible. **Whatever stage of the sale you are in, your goal is always to get to the next stage.** This attitude also enables you to maintain control of the sale, because **you always have control of the sale as long as the customer wants to keep going.** You keep the sale moving by giving the customer a desire to keep going. This book will show you how to do that for each stage of the sale.

The champions of new home sales cherish momentum. As a result, they are never the ones who stop the sale. **Only the customer should stop the sale, never the salesperson.** This principle sounds so obvious. Of course the salesperson should never stop the sale. Why would we ever do that? Actually there are a number of reasons.

Sometimes we are discouraged by the customer's demeanor when they first walk in the door. They seem unmotivated, so we decide not to waste our time. The sale never even gets started. But maybe the only reason they are not motivated is that we have not yet given them a reason to be. Customers won't be motivated to buy our homes until they want one, and that's where we come in.

Perhaps we are discouraged because the customer isn't giving us any buying signals. But as with motivation, buying signals often take time to blossom.

We may inadvertently stop the sale because we are bored with the repetition of our presentation. But it's not repetitious for the customer. They are hearing it for the first time.

Sometimes we may stop the sale simply because we're tired or distracted or not in a great frame of mind. There can be many reasons why we might stop the sale without even realizing it. But we know that when we're at our best we are focused on advancing each sale from one stage to the next until the customer buys a home or reaches a point where they can't go any farther that day. We have to keep our own frame of mind simple and positive: **"If the customer is still here, I'll take that as a yes."**

It's all about momentum. Momentum is magic in new home sales.

Think Of Selling As a Science and an Art

Another way to think about the basics and magic of selling is this: **Selling is a science, and it is also an art.** Great salespeople master them both. Let's look a little closer at what we mean when we say that selling is a science and an art, so we can understand how the basics of selling go hand in hand with the magic.

You sell at your best when you're enjoying it, and you gain the most enjoyment from selling when you're at your best. If you know how to get the most joy out of selling, it becomes easier to be a great salesperson.

The way to get the most joy out of selling is to learn how to do it well, and then to take what you've learned and develop a style that is uniquely your own. This means taking the science of selling (the basics) and creating a unique work of art (the magic) that only you could imagine. When you can accomplish this you will know the highest joy of selling, and you will be the salesperson your customers have been hoping to meet.

Who is the greatest artist of all time? That could be debated forever, but many people would say Leonardo da Vinci. If you asked who was the greatest scientist among the masters of art, Leonardo's name would come up again. He was a great artist because he was a great scientist. He had a passion for learning. He studied biology, physics, chemistry, engineering, and a variety of other sciences, as well as mathematics. His works of art and his many inventions have had more impact on our world today because of the way he applied science to his art.

In new home sales, the science is how you develop the skill and knowledge to master your craft. It provides the foundation for the customer's buying experience. It defines the selling process. It makes you a strong salesperson who can have a positive impact every time. The skills of selling are where you gain the confidence you convey to your customers, giving them the confidence that they've come to the right place.

The art turns skill into style. It enables us to provide an experience that is unique and wonderful. Our selling process needs to be consistent in order to stay at a high level, but the art is how we express the process in a distinctive way that provides a special joy. It also helps us connect with our customers in a more meaningful way. It makes our selling more effective and more fun.

Enjoy a Competitive Spirit

Some sales seem to just happen, but many are won or lost based on performance. A competitive spirit energizes your sales efforts, and that energy is part of the magic of selling. People don't become the best by accident. They become the best by wanting to be the best, and by wanting it more than their competition.

A competitive spirit arouses the desire to improve every day. You compete not only against the competition, but against your own standard. You enjoy testing yourself in order to increase your motivation, improve your skills and expand your comfort zone.

The desire to win is one of the defining characteristics of champions. However, a true competitive spirit is not characterized by the desire to win, but by the desire to compete. If you are truly competitive, it is the joy of competing that stimulates you, not just the joy of winning. Of course you want to win. You love to win. But you love to compete even if you don't win. You embrace losing as an opportunity to improve.

Champions sometimes lose, but they have a better way of processing it. The experience of losing motivates them instead of discouraging them. It helps build them up instead of breaking them down. It helps them grow and keeps them moving forward. Losing to an opponent arouses their curiosity. ("What did the opponent do better that enabled them to beat me?...Do they have strengths that I need to develop?... What can I do to beat them next time?") They may even feel a different kind of joy for their opponent's victory. After all, winning is always good, even when someone else is doing the winning. Champions do not view defeat as final, but merely as a rite of passage.

You win sales by doing a better job of:
- Providing each customer with an enriching and enjoyable experience – every step of the way
- Establishing connections with your customers, making them feel wanted, understanding their needs, and establishing a shared purpose for getting them where they want to go
- Understanding, believing and expressing your market position, your value, and your competitive advantages
- Demonstrating your homes and sites
- Handling objections and solving your customers' problems
- Achieving resolution and closing
- Following up

This book will help you to develop each of these competitive advantages, and it will help you win sales by developing the best mental approach as well as the best skills.

Conclusion

At the end of each chapter we will suggest ways to take what you have learned and bring it to life.

In this chapter we outlined ten priorities for discovering and mastering the magic of selling new homes. You have to thoroughly absorb them in order to gain their full power. Before you begin the next chapter, write one sentence (or more if you need to) that summarizes what each of these priorities means to you.

1. Make sure you have the passion.
2. Connect with your customers.
3. Be the salesperson they are looking for.
    a. Confidence
    b. Enthusiasm
    c. Joy
    d. Relaxation
    e. Purpose
4. Seek to achieve resolution.
5. Assume the leadership role.
6. Sell to customers as though they will buy.
7. Make customers feel wanted.
8. Don't stop the sale.
9. Think of selling as a science and an art.
10. Enjoy a competitive spirit.

Turning Basics into Magic

Before we begin combining the basics and the magic to create your selling style, we have one more vital piece of the foundation to install. Our next chapter will look at how to get yourself into the ideal frame of mind for selling – how to develop the strongest attitudes for the mental side of new home sales.

The Basics and the Magic

Chapter 2

THE MENTAL SIDE OF SELLING

We are writing this book in 2008. The market is tough – really tough. The mental side of selling is more important than ever. Of course, the right attitude will always make you more successful. But in tough times, having the right attitude outranks even skill and experience as a make-or-break characteristic for success. Notice that we didn't say a *good* attitude, we said the *right* attitude. A good attitude helps, but it may not be enough. To achieve success in new home sales over the long haul, through good times and bad, you need to have the right temperament, the right perspective, the right mindset. This is what we mean when we say the right attitude.

In this chapter we will explore the attitudes that take a new home salesperson to the highest level. We will describe the temperaments, perspectives and mindsets that will help you get the most out of every sales opportunity you have. The mental side of selling is where the basics and the magic come together, each enriching the other to make them both more powerful.

Here are nine ways of thinking that will take you to the top and keep you there.

Be Resolution Oriented

In our last chapter we talked about how important it is to have a temperament for seeking resolution. People who are driven to achieve resolution are well-suited to the sales profession. The pursuit of resolution makes you curious about finding answers, and then understanding those answers. You are curious about people, and about what motivates them. What are they trying to achieve, and why? Why are they looking for a new home? What kind of home are they looking for? What kinds of things are important to them in a home, a community, a location, a builder or a salesperson? What is it about their current home that dissatisfies them? How will they know when they have found the home that will make them say, "This is the one"? How will they know when their search is over – their mission completed?

Seeking resolution makes you more interested in your customers. The more interested you are in them, the better you will be able to connect with them.

A resolution-oriented temperament causes you to focus on decisions, and helps you lead the decision process. A customer has one ultimate goal in searching for a home – to resolve which home will most improve their lives. You have one ultimate goal – to help them resolve which home will most improve their lives. The desire to achieve this resolution is your most important common ground with your customers. A resolution-oriented temperament is always seeking to close loops and bring decisions to a conclusion. When this is your attitude toward selling, closing becomes the easiest part.

In our next chapter, "Getting the Sale Started," we will see how a resolution-oriented temperament shapes your greeting through the kinds of questions you ask and through your responses to their behavior. Then we will see how this same mindset eases you into a leadership position and guides your customers through the rest of the selling process.

Be Purposeful

People who seek resolution tend to be purposeful, but it is not the same characteristic. People who are purposeful tackle adversity better, because tough times can threaten our sense of purpose, and can destroy it if it is weak. A stronger sense of purpose produces greater courage, optimism and perseverance – a drive to do whatever it takes. It helps you conquer feelings of fear, doubt and helplessness.

When you feel a strong sense of purpose you feel more motivated and more energized. Nothing can stop you. You arrive at work believing you're going to sell a home, and knowing how you're going to do it. You take charge of every selling opportunity by creating a *spirit of shared purpose*, and then leading the quest to fulfill that purpose. This is how it feels to be a great salesperson. It's how you feel when you're at your best. By the end of this book you will enjoy an attitude and selling style in which these feelings come easily, if they do not already. Our next point will get you started.

Have a Momentum Mentality

In new home sales, momentum does not just happen. It is a way of thinking. Even when you are not thinking about momentum consciously, you think about it subconsciously. When you are "in the zone" – those wonderful times when you seem to do everything right – you're thinking momentum, consciously or subconsciously. Momentum is a mindset, and you want to keep that mindset active as much as possible. How do you make it happen?

In Chapter One we said that "momentum is one of the main ingredients in the magic of selling." Now let's revisit momentum as a mindset. We have already used the phrase, *"Don't stop the sale."* In a momentum mindset, **your goal is always to get the customer wanting to do one more thing.** You also assume that's what the customer wants. After all, they're still there, aren't they? But we cannot expect them to drive the momentum machine. They don't know how. It would be like asking them to drive a bulldozer.

How do you keep the customer wanting to do one more thing? By creating a sense of positive anticipation for that next thing. They want to keep going. With a momentum mentality, you are always thinking one step ahead and creating enthusiasm in the buyer's mind for what lies ahead. You execute each stage of the sale with the next stage clearly in mind. The purpose of each stage is to set up the next stage. The purpose of each decision is to set up the next decision.

Think of the selling process as a baseball diamond. When you have learned the customer's situation and conveyed your basic selling message, you have made it to first base – a single. A double would be when they pick a favorite house type. When they pick a favorite home site, it's a triple. It's a home run when you get the contract. As long as the ball is still rolling, you keep running to the next base, and the ball is still rolling as long as the customer is still there. You should assume the customer wants to keep going until they tell you they don't. Take the attitude that reasonable people don't postpone improving their lives.

Of course, you want to hit a home run every time, but a triple should be a realistic goal for every viable prospect on their first visit. Even if you don't get a home run on the first visit, a triple is still a good hit, and the more triples you hit the more runs you will score. Triples get customers to the point where they have a fairly complete picture of your total package. They may need to go home and process it (we'll come to that in our chapter on closing), but at least they are engaged enough in your community that they have become a serious prospect on their first visit, even in a tough market. Always go for a triple with every customer who could possibly buy a home at your community. Once they're on third, go for the close.

Always think momentum. It's an essential part of the mental side of selling.

Help Customers Complete Their Thoughts

We need to know what our customers think. But more importantly, *they* need to know what they think. One of the most rewarding services you can provide, for them as well as for you, is to help your customers figure out what they really think. This is one of the most important, and also most overlooked, opportunities that the selling process provides. But what does it mean?

Customers come to us with a mass (and mess) of partial thoughts. They have the beginnings of a variety of ideas, but the ideas are not fully developed. Before they complete one thought, they jump to another. In most cases this is because they don't know how to finish their thoughts. They have not yet learned enough, and they are still looking for a mentor they can trust.

For example, buyers in 2008 know it's a tough market, but they don't know if that means it's a good time to buy or a bad time. What if the market continues to get worse? What will happen with the sale of their current home? They know they want a good deal, but they're not sure what a good deal is. Is it the lowest price, the largest discount, the most standard features? They know they want a large lot, but they don't know if they are willing to pay more or accept tradeoffs in order to get it. They know they want to back up to trees, but they don't want to pay a lot premium.

When we feel as though a customer's thoughts are going in the wrong direction, our first instinct may be to stop their thought process dead in its tracks – to nip the problem before it gets out of control. However, this can be a perilous trap. Yes, we want to lead and we want to sell, but we also have to help buyers resolve their own confusion by allowing their thoughts to follow a complete course until they have reached a conclusion.

For example, suppose they feel anxious about the market. Before trying to convince them that now is the time to buy, ask them, *"How do you feel about buying in this market?... What is it that brought you into the market at this time?...What is it that will make you say, 'My journey is over, my mission is complete?'...If you found a home that would really make you happy, what would you do?"* You can get them to reflect on what they have already experienced and also learn how they want to be sold by asking, *"How have you enjoyed your house-hunting experience (adventure) so far? (How has your search been going so far?)"* Get them to decide what they really think and feel, and then to express it so they can understand it as well as you. Often people don't fully understand what they think or how they feel until they try to put it into words.

If they seem obsessed with getting the best deal, learn more about what they think before trying to assure them that you have the best deal. Ask them, *"How will you know when you've gotten the best deal?"* Can they even afford your home? *"If you take the deal and the market out of the equation, is this a price you feel you can afford?"*

For the larger lot: *"Is a large home site a must, or could you live with a smaller site if you could get more home for the same money?"*

For the lot premium, you could mix a question with a statement. *"Think of premium home sites just as you would any other upgrade. If the site is larger or it's on a cul-de-sac or it backs up to trees or open space, it has a higher value, just like carpeting or cabinets or counter tops. Is the home site a priority, or are other upgrades more important?"*

Before trying to resolve an issue that is frustrating them, help them to decide how they really feel about it. They will appreciate that you are truly interested, and you will begin to establish that all-important connection of shared purpose in finding the home that is the best total balance of features for the price they can afford.

You have to know their needs in order to fulfill them. At the same time, remember that their needs are a moving target, a work in progress. Their needs and priorities evolve as their search for a home progresses. Along the way, they need encouragement, direction, reassurance and resolution with the help of an expert they can trust. They need someone to help them clarify their own thoughts and feelings. They need your help in order to decide where they really want to go and how they plan to get there.

If it seems to you that a customer is walking around in circles in the dark, it probably feels that way to them, too. When they get derailed by fear, confusion or negativity, they need help finding their way back to their original mission of improving their lives. When they come to your sales office in a negative or frustrated frame of mind, get excited about turning them around with an experience that exceeds their expectations. Don't be shy about asking questions that will help them to probe more deeply into their own true priorities and to express the obstacles that may be standing in their way.

Know, Understand and Embrace Your Market Position

Every purchaser of every product on earth has one question that is more important to them than any other. However, they rarely come right out and ask it. In fact, they may not even consciously realize the question, because it is programmed so deeply within them. But the question is always there, and until it is answered the customer's comfort level will always be a little off. The question is this: **Why do other people buy your product?** Another way of wording it is, **Why do people choose you over everyone else?** The answer to these questions is your market position, and it needs to be expressed in a way your customers will understand.

Staying connected with your market position is an important part of the mental side of selling. Salespeople sometimes allow market position to slip to the back of their minds because they are trying to focus on the customers' needs. After all, market position is an internal corporate matter, so it doesn't really have anything to do with the customer, right? Why should the customer care what your market position is? All they care about is whether the home will fulfill their needs. But customers also need to know why others have chosen your homes. This can help them prioritize their needs.

Even if you are at the beginning of a community and do not yet have a sales track record, you can explain your market position as a mission statement – why you believe people will buy your homes – what gives your homes the competitive edge.

We will go into detail about how this works in our next chapter on "Getting the Sale Started." For our purposes here in talking about the mental side of selling, the point is to make sure your mind is focused on why people *will* buy your homes as opposed to why they won't. Know your competitive position in the market place so you can explain why your homes are the best for the money.

Make sure you believe that your market position is strong enough to achieve your goals. If you believe it is not, then this issue needs to be resolved. You need to believe that your position is strong enough to win your share of sales as long as customers experience your homes in the right way. The whole purpose of a market position is to win sales. If you do not understand, believe and express your position well enough, sales will be lost. Learning a customer's needs and fulfilling those needs is vital. But conveying your market position to the customer will validate the rational part of the buying decision as well as the emotional part.

Believe That You Have the Position of Strength

One of the dangerous attitudes we can fall into is the notion that the customer holds the position of strength. This mindset becomes even more treacherous when the customer also believes they hold the stronger position, which is most likely to happen in a tough market. Here is the best way to resolve this mindset.

The customer does have the position of strength if they don't want your home. The market has nothing to do with it. But if they don't want your home, position of strength doesn't matter anyway. The balance will only shift in your favor after customers have decided they want your home, so you focus on getting them interested in your home. Then everything changes.

Once the customer wants your home, the position of strength shifts to you, and here's why. **Once they reach the point where they want your home more than they want any other, you have the position of strength because you can sell the home to someone else, but they can only buy it from you.** You can provide encouragement and reassurance to the customer, but if they are not up to the task, you'll have other opportunities.

You absolutely must be committed to this concept. If you aren't, you won't be able to project the kind of confidence the customer needs to see in order to maintain their confidence that buying your home is the right decision. If they do consider buying from you when they believe you are selling from fear or weakness, the chances are high that you will wind up with one of three results:

1. They will get cold feet and decide not to sign a contract.

2. They will sign a contract, but continue trying to renegotiate after the contract is ratified.
3. They will sign a contract, but then get buyer's remorse and try to back out of it.

It is not just your confidence that is at stake with your attitude, it is their confidence as well.

Keep It Simple

Making the customer's experience with you more enjoyable than it is with anyone else will give you a competitive advantage. Your attitude should be, "Selling homes is fun for me, and I want to make it fun for the customer." One way to make their experience more enjoyable is to make it feel easy.

For starters, you want your own mind to be as clear as possible – free from clutter, especially anxiety and negativity. Replace the clutter with thoughts like this: *"Here comes a customer who's looking for a new home. I can't wait to learn about them, and help them learn about us. I know why people choose my homes over everyone else's; I know why they choose me over every other salesperson; and I'm not going to stop the sale."* That is clearheaded selling!

The more clearheaded you are in your approach to selling, the more successful you will be. In selling, simplicity is your friend, complexity your enemy. You must never create complexity. When you are faced with it, your goal is to simplify it. Simplicity is important in new home sales because it helps customers make decisions. The more complicated a decision becomes, the more difficult it is to make. Making decisions with confidence requires uncluttered thinking. You must help customers to simplify their thoughts and maintain their focus in order to help them make decisions with conviction. For many customers buying a home is very complicated. It is not the kind of decision they make very often, and they are not experts at it. As a salesperson, your mission is to take that which is complex and make it simple. As we begin discussing the selling process in the next chapter, we will include techniques for helping customers to clear their heads, stay focused on their mission, and get back on track when they are derailed.

Understand What Urgency Really Is, and Have the Right Attitude About It

Urgency has become a perplexing topic in new home sales, so we'll spend some time here digging into what it really means and how it is created.

Give Urgency Time to Develop

Sometimes we want to see urgency in our customers too soon, and when we don't, we get discouraged. For example, let's suppose we ask about a customer's time frame for buying and they say, "We'll probably do something in about a year." Our internal response is, "Oh, man, another customer with no urgency." But what does their comment really mean? Think how many customers say that. Why are all these people coming in today with the intention of buying in a year? It doesn't make sense. What does a year really mean? Is it 365 days? Is it somewhere between nine and fifteen months? There's something else going on. When customers say, "I'm looking in a year," assume that what they're really saying is, *"I can't decide on a timetable until I find a home I want."*

This is actually a reasonable approach for a customer to take. Suppose you ask a twenty-two-year old, "How soon do you want to get married?" If they have not yet met someone they want to marry, they might respond, "I want to be about thirty." But if they meet the love of their life the next day, they might revise their timetable. Their "urgency" to get married does not begin until they find a person they want to marry. The urgency to buy a home does not begin until the home that will improve life is discovered.

If a customer is being transferred, or has already sold their current home, or has a lease that is about to expire, they have a circumstance which drives their urgency to make a decision on a deadline. If there is only one home that meets their needs, and someone else is also interested in the same home, that creates urgency as well. But most of the time, urgency to make a change is driven by a desire to improve our lives. Until we believe that taking action will improve our lives, there is no urgency to act. But once we believe the action *will* improve our lives, then our thought process changes to, "The sooner I act, the sooner my life will improve." Now we have urgency to act.

Most customers do not have pre-existing urgency to buy when they first walk in your door. Their urgency will develop as the selling process progresses. In his book, *Selling with Momentum,* Richard Tiller identifies a seven-step process of how urgency develops for many customers.

1. The customers are dissatisfied with their current home.
2. They must want your home.

3. They must believe your home is the best available in your market.
4. They must pick one home and site from those you have available.
5. They must realize that their favorite could be someone else's favorite, too.
6. They must believe they are in the right place at the right time.
7. They must believe that the sooner they act, the sooner their lives will improve.

When a customer expresses no urgency in the beginning with such comments as, "I'm just looking," or, "I just wanted to see your decorating," or, "I have a friend who may be moving to the area," or, "We might do something in about a year," what they're really saying is, "I don't expect to find the home of my dreams at your community." And why should they? Most of us don't believe life can be that simple. We believe we have to keep looking and looking in order to find what we want. But once we do find what we want, everything can change quickly. That is why so many people who start out saying, "I'm looking in a year," wind up buying in a month – or a week.

If a customer at first acts standoffish, aloof, unfocused, unmotivated, or perhaps even rude, consider this perspective. Instead of thinking, "Another tire kicker," think, "You have no interest? You have no motivation? You have no urgency? You don't even like me? That's perfect! I wouldn't have it any other way. I don't want you to like me until you know me, and that will take five minutes. I don't want you to be interested until you know what I'm selling and why other people buy it, and that could take another five minutes. I don't want you to be motivated until you want what I'm selling, and that could take half an hour. I don't want you to feel any urgency until you've picked out your favorite of my homes, and that could take an hour. So let's get started."

However reluctant, ambivalent, bewildered, anxiety-ridden or unmotivated they may be, your customer has already overcome those traits enough to visit your community. You may not know what is going on in their mind, but you do know that **they came to you, you didn't go to them.**

Urgency Grows Out of Confidence

We often think that urgency grows out of fear, especially fear of loss. You should always take advantage of any opportunity you have to bring fear of loss into play as a closing tool. Step five of the seven-step urgency process stated above is, "They must realize that their favorite could be someone else's favorite, too."

The fear of loss may be about the loss of their favorite home or home site to another buyer, or it could be about the loss of a limited-time incentive, or of the opportunity to select an optional item because the cutoff is imminent. We have all made decisions due to fear of loss – the fear that if we do not act, we may lose an opportunity.

We also need to appreciate that urgency can come from the opposite direction. Urgency often grows out of confidence. We feel urgency to do something because we feel confident that we will do it successfully, and that after we do it we will be better off than we were before. The more confident we feel that a decision or action will improve our lives, the more urgency we feel to complete it.

We need to sell in a way that keeps raising the confidence level of our customers, so they will feel more empowered to make decisions and take action. How do we increase their confidence through our selling? We do it in the following ways.

- We convey our own confidence, which becomes contagious.
- We convey our enthusiasm, which also becomes contagious.
- We connect with customers, being sincerely interested in them and in learning and fulfilling their needs. In this way we are able to connect with them on the deepest level for selling – the level of shared purpose.
- We sell to customers as though they will buy.
- We convey a strong selling message.
- We lead customers from one decision to the next.
- We help them to feel that buying our home will improve their lives.

Lack of motivation and urgency are not a disease we treat. They are merely symptoms of the disease of lack of confidence, purpose and direction. If we can help our customers to strengthen their confidence and their sense of purpose, and then provide them with the direction they need to keep moving forward, their motivation and urgency will take care of itself. Later chapters will explain how to do this in each stage of the sale.

Embrace the Joy of Improving

If you want to do an honest check on your own level of motivation, what is the truest way to measure it? Is it by your energy and enthusiasm? Perhaps your desire to succeed? As valuable as these assets are, the truest sign of motivation is the desire to improve. **"IMPROVE" is the number one word in the vocabulary of success.** An example of motivation in its purest form is a person who keeps striving to improve – even on days when they don't have energy or enthusiasm, but only the faith that if they keep improving, their success will take care of itself.

One of the greatest benefits of the desire to improve is the unique joy it brings. Improving brings a special satisfaction because it is the result of your own initiative and perseverance. When you are improving at an endeavor, you enjoy it more. When you enjoy it more, you continue to improve. The pursuit of excellence can be a wonderful source of joy, satisfaction and fulfillment before the success itself has even been achieved. This is because the improvements you make along the way can be as emotionally rewarding as the ultimate success.

Begin each day by asking, "What will I do today to be better than I was yesterday?" At the end of each day ask, "What did I do better today than I did yesterday?" You may even want to keep a daily journal of improvement initiatives to make this exercise even more powerful.

Improving creates a momentum of its own, because the joy of improving makes you want to improve more. However, it begins as an act of will. You need will and courage to step outside of your comfort zone in order to improve. The reward is that your comfort zone expands. Don't deprive yourself of the satisfaction of stretching, of stepping out of your comfort zone, expanding your reach, being better today than you were yesterday. Don't let these opportunities pass you by.

Conclusion

In this chapter we discussed nine ways to get your mind clear, quiet, focused and sharp for new home sales. When your mind is in this state you will be able to enrich the basics of selling with your own special magic. You will create stronger relationships, have greater impact, and sell more homes. You will achieve success, but also something more – you will achieve mastery.

Now let's bring these nine mindsets to life. Before beginning Chapter Three, complete the following exercises to begin making these mindsets your own.

Rate your temperament in the following three categories on a scale of one to ten. Then write down one thought you can add to your mindset or one action you can take to lift yourself a notch higher in each category. (The reason we are asking you to come up with your own answers as opposed to providing examples for you is so you can activate this part of your mind independently. Later throughout this book we will provide examples of how these thought processes come into play during the sale.)

1. *Resolution oriented.*
2. *Purposeful.*
3. *Momentum mentality.*

Write down what the following mindset means to you at this point:

4. *Help customers complete their thoughts.*

Are you confident that you:

5. *Know, understand and embrace the market position of your community.*

Can you express it? That is to say, can you make a concise statement of ways in which you offer the most home for the money? Do you feel that your competitive position is strong enough to achieve your company's goals?

6. *Believe that you have the position of strength.*

Repeat the following sentence to yourself out loud: "Once my customers want my home, I have the position of strength, because I can sell the home to someone else, but they can only buy it from me."

7. *Keep it simple.*

Can you remember a time when a customer made a sale more complicated than it needed to be? What did you do (or what could you have done) to make it less complicated?

Can you think of a time when *you* made a sale more complicated than it needed to be? Is there any way you could have made it simpler?

Repeat the following four statements to yourself, and then write out the appropriate information relating to each statement.

    a. "I love to sell homes." {Why do you love to sell homes?}
    b. "I know why people choose my homes." {Why do people choose your homes? This is the market position issue we discussed.}
    c. "I know why people choose me over every other salesperson." {Why do people prefer to buy from you?}
    d. "I won't stop the sale." {Name one thing you can do to keep the sale moving.}

8. *Create urgency through confidence.*

List three new ways you can help your customers feel more confident about buying a home at your community.

9. *Embrace the joy of improving.*

Write down one thing you can improve in order to become a better salesperson.

Now that we have seen where the magic of selling comes from, and how to get mentally prepared to tap into its full power, let's see how to combine the basics and the magic – the science and the art – to create a high-impact selling style, beginning with the greeting and proceeding through the sale to the close.

Chapter 3
GETTING THE SALE STARTED

Here comes a customer – it's show time! All you need is skill and magic, and you've got them both. Now let's bring them to life and sell a home!

First, remember the five traits customers need to see in you to make the magic happen: confidence, enthusiasm, joy, relaxation and purpose. Now you're ready!

When you first greet a customer, make sure you are relaxed and smiling. Relaxation produces comfort and confidence. Smiling says to a customer, "I'm glad you're here." And you sure are, because they want to buy a home. They may not be ready to buy a home, but don't worry about that yet. For now, all that matters is that they want to buy a home – somewhere, sometime, somehow.

Sell to them as though they will buy, and you will give them a better experience. You always want to be aware of what the customer is experiencing. See the interaction from their perspective. This awareness gives you more warmth and energy, and it helps you connect with your customers.

The First Few Minutes

The basics of selling say that you begin your interaction with each customer by:

- Introducing yourself
- Learning a little about them and what they are looking for
- Telling them a little about yourself and what you are selling
- Beginning to connect with them by establishing a sense of shared purpose

The magic says you do it with:

- Enthusiasm for your work as well as your customer
- Sincere interest in who they are and what is best for them
- A strong sense of purpose for helping them to fulfill their mission of improving their lives with a new home

The basics make you good. The magic makes you special.

If at first the customer seems cool toward you, don't be discouraged. There could be any number of reasons for a cool demeanor. They may simply not be warm by nature, or they may not be comfortable in your environment. That's okay, because as important as warmth is in a business relationship, it is not as important as trust. As for the customer, they did not come in looking for a friend, they came in looking for a home, and they are facing an intimidating situation. If they don't warm up to you at first, it's not the end of the world. When they learn to trust you, the warmth will develop.

In your first few minutes with customers, showing interest in them as people will mean more to them than trying to sell them a home. But the first leads to the second quite easily. For example, after you have introduced yourself, exchanged names, and told them you're glad they're here, ask them where they live. Everyone is comfortable talking about their home town. Show interest in where they are from – and in everything they tell you from that point on – and soon you're off and running. Remember, don't just listen to what customers tell you, also respond with interest. That demonstrates that you are listening, and that you care about what they are telling you.

Begin With a Plan

When you create your greeting style, you should be consistent whenever possible in order to insure that you always perform at your highest level. The primary purpose of the greeting is to get the sale started – to get it off the ground. It should unfold as a prepared sequence that keeps the exchange of information moving forward. While learning their needs and priorities, you are also beginning to show what makes your homes special.

Here is one example of a greeting sequence that starts out with a social feeling to it and then develops into a business conversation.* It keeps the interaction human and natural, and reminds us of the adage, *"Don't let the customer see you selling."*

---

*Several of the techniques described in this book have been discussed previously in Rich Tiller's book, *Selling with Momentum*. We are including them again here among our examples of the basics not to be repetitious, but because they have stood the test of time.

- "Hi, I'm _____ [Wait for them to respond with their names.]... *It's a pleasure to meet you. Thanks for coming out. Do you folks live nearby? (or, Where are you folks coming from? or, Are you folks from this area?)* [Show your interest in wherever they are currently living, depending on how much you know about the area.]... *How long have you lived there?...How have you enjoyed it?... Are you thinking of making a move?... What is it that's gotten you thinking about moving?* [This is your first true business question, since it begins to delve into their motivation and sense of purpose. From this point on, your questions evolve easily and naturally into "qualifying" questions.]... *Do you have a particular time frame in mind?...* [If necessary you can follow up with:] *Is there anything driving your timetable?... Have you decided yet on a price you don't want to go above?...* [Again, if necessary:] *How did you arrive at that number?"*

If the customers have a clear sense of purpose and a desire to talk about it right away, they will appreciate and enjoy your questions, and you can keep asking more questions as long as they are receptive. You will want to have these questions at your fingertips. Examples of a few more would be:

- "*Where are you in the process?*"
- "*Why are you looking?*" [This could be used in place of the question, "*What is it that's gotten you thinking about moving?*"]
- "*Are you just beginning your search, or have you been looking for awhile?*"
- "*How has your search been going so far?...Have you seen anything you've liked? (Tell me what you've seen that you've liked.)*"

- *"Are you familiar with this area?... How do you like it?... Does this location work for you?... Are you considering any other areas?"* [Your question about whether they are familiar with the area can lead into an overview of your location. Remember that your location is one of the most important elements in your package, so be sure every customer fully appreciates the benefits of your location. Then you can also ask if they are familiar with your community and your builder.]
- *"What sorts of things are important to you in a location?"*
- *"Do you work in this area? (Where do you work?)... What kind of work do you do?"*
- *"Are you planning to sell your current home?... Do you have it on the market yet?"*
- *"What kind of home do you live in now?...How do you like it?... Are you looking for something different?... In what ways do you want your next home to be different than the one you live in now?"*
- *"Do you have a particular kind of home in mind that you're looking for?... Is there anything that's a top priority for you?"*
- *"Do you have any special activities or interests that will be a factor in the kind of home (community) you choose?"*
- *"How are you feeling about the whole idea of moving?"*

Be Prepared To Switch Gears

The approaches suggested above are time-tested methods for greeting customers and getting a sale started – they are the basics. They help you get to know your customers and determine how to sell them a home. They are also designed to help you build rapport and a position of trusted leadership. If you can establish a greeting that consistently follows this pattern, you will sell more homes.

However, there is a pitfall, and in a tough market it can be a big one. The above approach assumes that your customer has a clearly defined sense of purpose and a desire to talk about it. In other words, it assumes a cooperative customer. But what if the customer doesn't want to talk to you? What if they don't have anything to say? How can you "sell as though they will buy" if they're not acting as though they will buy? No problem. Just switch gears.

Just because they may not be willing to talk doesn't mean they're not willing to listen. Many customers want to know what's going on before they start answering questions. You certainly have plenty to say, and now is a great time to start saying it. It is also a great time to bring into play the "No urgency? That's perfect!" attitude we discussed in Chapter Two.

When a customer says, "We're just looking," or, "We just want to look at your decorating," it doesn't mean anything negative or disheartening. It just means, "We don't have anything to say to you – yet." Many customers are unenthusiastic at first simply because they don't expect to find the home of their dreams at your community. They're not willing to invest anything, including conversation, until they have more reason to hope. Why should they believe they will find the perfect home in the next hour? How many guys walk into a singles bar with an engagement ring in their pocket? Life isn't supposed to be that easy. But sometimes it is. As soon as they see something at your community that interests them, everything can change quickly. Sell as though you have what they're looking for. You just have to help them get interested.

Plan A is to connect with your customers and learn their needs by asking questions. If Plan A didn't work, switch to Plan B. Plan B is to give them an overview of what you're selling, and come back to your questions later.

Suppose a customer says, "We just want to look at your model," and their tone implies, "We want to see it alone." You decide to let them go alone, at least at first, to give them some space before you rejoin them in a few minutes. Say to them, *"Before you get started, let me give you a quick overview of what we're doing here."* Or you could put it in the form of a question: *"Before you get started, would you like a quick overview of what we're doing here?"* If they say no, that's a clear indication of the lowest possible level of interest or motivation, at least in the beginning.

However, for the customer who is reluctant to talk but willing to listen, a *Brief Initial Overview* of your community is the best way to get your foot in the door by getting their attention. In fact, your *Brief Initial Overview* is so important it deserves a nickname, so let's call it by its initials – BIO. Once you have gotten as far as you can with your initial questions, switch gears to your BIO. Your BIO helps you create interest. What is your BIO, and what is the best way to convey it your customers?

Your BIO is a short, high-impact summary of your most important selling points – what your customers need to know initially in order to appreciate the advantages of what you are offering. Your BIO can include basic information about the location, the community (its size, amenities, aesthetics, etc.), the home sites, the product or the builder – the major highlights that can be summarized in a few minutes. The most important element in your BIO is your selling message.

The Selling Message

Your selling message expresses your market position. In Chapter Two when we discussed market position we said that every customer's number one question is, *"Why do other people buy your homes?"* The answer to this question is your market position. To develop a selling message, begin by trying to put your market position into a sentence or two. Create a short statement that explains why customers have chosen you over others in the past, or why you feel they will choose you in the future. In what ways are you special? In what ways are you the best of all the alternatives currently available to your customers?

Your selling message is your basic mission statement. It gives your customers a way to separate your homes from everyone else's before they even see your model. It helps shape their thought process about what you are selling. It carves out your own particular space in their mind. It causes them to think differently about you than they think about everyone else. It tells them why they should consider your home. It motivates them to pay attention to your homes – and even to like them – right from the start. Getting customers to look at your homes in a different and special way is part of the magic of selling.

Your selling message is an important way to create interest in your homes and build rapport with your customers. For customers who are reluctant to talk but willing to listen, your selling message can actually be a great way to establish rapport. If you can create interest in what you are selling, rapport will often take care of itself. Creating interest engages customers just as much as creating rapport does, so interest leads to rapport just as much as rapport leads to interest. Your selling message can be a vehicle for connecting with customers when other efforts to build rapport don't work. If they are interested in your information, they'll be willing to talk.

Your selling message helps shape your customers' perspective. When customers first visit your community, they will perceive things from whatever point of view they brought with them – through whatever perspective they have developed from their past experiences. Their perspective may be shaped partly by what they have seen or read or been told by well-meaning advisors, or by what your competitors have told them is important in order to make their homes appear more favorable. For this reason it is vital that customers hear your selling message *before* they begin the model tour, so they will be able to see your homes from your point of view. Seeing your homes from your point of view, and the point of view of your builder, is the only way customers can fully appreciate what you are offering.   Only you can create the initial feeling that you have something different, special and better than anything else in your market for your price.

The selling message is only a minute or two of your BIO, but think of it as a springboard for the rest of your presentation. It does not take the place of identifying and fulfilling the customer's needs; however, it complements need fulfillment by helping to retrain the customer's thought process. It helps them understand how your home not only meets their needs, but also provides the best quality of life for the money. You may occasionally be fortunate enough to offer a home that perfectly matches the customer's ideal. But when this is not the case (which is most of the time), the competitive aspect of selling comes into play. Your selling message is what helps you establish your competitive advantage as early as possible. It also helps you to have greater impact throughout the rest of your sale.

A selling message is not a laundry list of features, or even advantages. It is a brief statement of the message you feel will have the highest impact on your customers in terms of the differences that make your homes and community special. Here are a few examples of a basic selling message.

- *"Our homes cost a little more, but we give a lot more. Our homeowners tell us we offer a better total package for the money. We include nicer features inside our homes, and you'll also see the difference in our exteriors and in the overall community. Once they see it all, many people tell us they expected our homes to cost more than they do."*
- *"For $300,000 we offer the best value of any homes around – hands down. When I say best value, what I mean is…* [explain your community's unique definition of value]*."*
- *"A lot of people choose our homes because of the approach we take to architecture. We're known for more sophisticated designs than other builders in our price range."*
- *"These homes are built on smaller sites because if a large site isn't your top priority, then you can use the money you would have wasted on a larger site to get more home in a better location."*
- *"There's no other community around that provides the feeling of this one. It begins with the setting that surrounds us, and then once you enter the community it*

- *just keeps getting better. We put a lot of thought into the feeling of the community, and you see it right away in the streetscape."*
- *"People not only love our homes, but we also offer the nicest selection of home sites you will see in any new homes in this area."*
- *"These homes offer more square footage for the money than any other homes in our market."*
- *"What makes these townhomes special is that they feel like single family homes inside."*
- *"People love our homes, and the size of our home sites is competitive. But where we stand out the most is in the lifestyle package we offer. Our amenities at his community are second to none."*
- *"When we designed these homes, our goal was to put more space than you would expect in the rooms where you spend most of your time."*
- *"One of the reasons people choose these homes is they like the fact that we include features they didn't expect to see in this price range. We include features in $300,000 homes that people expect to see in a $500,000 home. It makes our homes cost a little more, but it makes them worth a lot more."*
- *"Our location here is amazing."* [Give details.]
- *"These homes are wonderfully affordable, and yet they still have everything you need. After taxes, they're less expensive per month than many of the rentals around."*

Keep the Conversation Interactive

When offering your BIO (including your selling message), make sure you don't talk too long. Give your customers another opportunity to get back into the conversation, even if they were reluctant to talk to you at first. After giving a brief overview that includes a few of your highest impact selling points, you can say, *"So that's a little bit about us. How about you, what's your situation?"* Or you can ask a question that relates to the information you have given them. Or you could simply try a tie-down: *"How does it sound so far?"*

If they are ready to start opening up, you can begin asking the questions you had wanted to ask earlier. If they are still reluctant to give you information about themselves, but seem attentive and impressed by what you are saying, you can continue down your BIO path by asking if they are familiar with your builder, your location, or some other piece of information they will find interesting.

Occasionally you will have a customer who doesn't want to cooperate in any way – talking or listening – until they have been through your model, and they absolutely insist on going alone. You try to catch up with them later, and they still want to be left alone. Keep giving it time. If they refuse to sign your guest card and sneak away without coming back to your office, don't lose any sleep over it, as long as it's not happening more than 10% of the time.

Once a customer is willing to interact, ask questions that determine their initial motivation, their primary needs and priorities, and their ability to buy.

Questions involving motivation include:

- *"How has your search (house-hunting adventure) been going so far?"*
- *"Have you decided yet on a time frame for moving?"*
- *"What is it that's gotten you thinking about moving?"*

This question is designed to uncover their level of discomfort in their current situation. If they insist that they're perfectly happy where they are, and they just want to see what's out there, you will need to ask them at later points in the presentation, *"How do you like this compared to where you're living now?"* If they continue to seem content with their current situation and are unmotivated to talk about moving, you may have to accept a low probability of making a sale. Customers need to feel enough dissatisfaction with their current situation to overcome their fear of buying and the inconvenience of moving. They have to be convinced that their lives will improve by purchasing your home. You need to learn about the source and level of their pain in order to provide the cure. Once you learn their pain, you can keep returning to it at later points in the sale. But if there is no pain, and if you are unable to create any, you may not have a bona fide prospect.

- *"How are you feeling about the whole idea of moving?"* Only ask this one if there seems to be ambivalence that needs to be discussed.

Questions involving needs and priorities include:

- *"Have you given much thought yet to the kind of home you're looking for?"*
- *"Do you have any top priorities (must haves) for your next home?"*
- *"Have you seen anything so far that you've liked?"*

Questions about their financial ability to buy would include:

- *"Is there a price or payment you can't (don't want to) go above?"*
- *"Have you talked to anyone yet about the financial end*

of buying a home? If it would be helpful, I can give you a five-minute crash course in the basics."
- *"Will you need to sell the place where you live now? Have you had any kind of appraisal on it yet?"*

Don't rush these questions. You're not "qualifying" the customer, you're learning about them. Some customers don't see any point in pursuing these kinds of conversations unless they want your home. They might start acting agitated if you keep asking these questions when they are reluctant to answer them before they want your home. Start out with these questions assuming the customer will be cooperative. If they have a sense of purpose and are trying to learn more, they will be happy to answer your questions. But if they don't cooperate, switch gears to creating interest, and come back to your questions later, after the customer begins to see that this might be the right place after all.

How do you help them to feel that they have found the right place? Of course, the main thing is for them to believe they've found the right home. But there's more to it, and this is where another part of the magic of selling comes back into play. It has to do with the way people make decisions, especially big ones.

The Three Elements of Decisions

When people make life-changing decisions (like the decision to get married, take a new job, or buy a new home), there are usually three elements that come into play – emotional, rational and intuitive. In most major decisions, the emotional element seems to come first. A person *desires* another person, a job or a home. In new home sales you arouse and nurture those feelings through emotional selling, which includes your own enthusiasm for your homes and for fulfilling the needs of your customers.

Next is the rational element of the decision process – *reassurance through reason* that what we want emotionally is also what is best for us. In new home sales, you activate the rational element by helping customers understand the reasons your home is better for them than any other home they have seen, and better for them than the home where they live now. While the emotional element may come first, the rational element usually needs to catch up in order for people to complete their decision with confidence.

On the surface, the emotional element and the rational element would seem to be all it takes to make a major decision correctly. However, the third element – the intuitive one – can sometimes be the most important of all. The intuitive element is the part of the decision in which the customer believes that "everything just feels right." For many customers, this is a vital part of their decision. It is as though an external confirmation is reassuring them that they are doing the right thing. Customers may express this feeling in just those words: "Of all the places we've visited, this is the place where everything just feels right." Or they may say, "I feel like this was meant to be," or, "I feel as though I was led to this," or, "There's good karma here." Many times they don't express it at all, but it's there just the same. It's as though a peaceful, comfortable assurance that they can't describe is validating their decision to buy your home.

How can you inspire that feeling? First, if customers see in you a sincere *joy of purpose*, they can be profoundly affected. Their own sense of purpose increases when you enthusiastically join forces with them to improve their lives. They gain confidence by seeing the joy you gain from getting them where they want to go. Customers do not often see this kind of joy in salespeople. When they do see it, the entire experience feels different. You need to radiate a feeling of, "I love my work, my homes, my company and my customers." If everything seems right with you, it must be right with your homeowners as well. When customers feel as though your world is good, they feel as though their world will be good, too.

Another way to make your community feel like the "right place" is to make your customers feel good about themselves. Sometimes we focus too much on trying to make our customers feel good about us. But if you can be the one who makes them feel good about themselves, they will reciprocate that feeling to you. They will also feel more empowered. When you help customers to feel good about themselves and empowered to act, they feel more confident about moving to the next step.

Make customers feel that they are the center of your world. We mentioned earlier how important it is to listen attentively to what they say, and to respond with interest. Much is said about the importance of listening in new home sales. But it is *responding* to what you hear that builds a closer relationship with customers. Respond in a way that makes them feel glad they interacted with you so they will want to interact more. Whenever possible, take something they have said and work it into future conversation.

We have said previously that the magic of selling comes partly from making customers feel wanted and partly from building their trust and confidence. Nurturing the intuitive element of their buying decision as well as the emotional and rational elements will help you get there. When you sell in a way that appeals to all three of these decision-making elements, you add one more kind of magic to your selling style.

Help Customers Complete Their Thoughts

In Chapter Two we discussed the importance of helping customers to fully understand their own thoughts and feelings – especially their motivations, anxieties and intentions. As important as it is to keep the sale moving forward, it is just as important not to rush it.

If customers express fear or ambivalence, either verbally or in their behavior, give them an opportunity to work through it while you are there to help them. Don't try to slip past the concerns in the hope that they will just go away. When you assume the leadership role in the relationship, this includes leading them through the thought process that will resolve their concerns and anxieties. You do this in much the same way a professional counselor does. You don't try to conquer them in a debate. You let them talk about what is bothering them, and you lead the direction of the conversation through your questions and suggestions.

The magic of selling includes leading the customer's efforts to achieve resolution. In order to resolve their buying decision, they must resolve areas of concern or confusion along the way. We gave several examples of this in Chapter Two, and here's one more.

Suppose a customer says, "I know people tell me it's better to own than rent, but I'm not so sure." Our first impulse may be to say, "It's definitely better to own, and here's why." However, it sounds like he's already been told that, but he's not yet convinced. Something is still bothering him. It's best to find out what that is, so you don't waste time trying to address the wrong problem. For example, you don't want to dwell on the investment benefits of ownership if he's already sold on them. Maybe his concern is the fear of change, or the hassle of moving, or fear of the responsibility of owning a home, or fear that he'll lose his job and default on his mortgage. Perhaps his concern is cash flow until his next annual tax refund, because he doesn't understand that he can adjust his exemptions. There are so many possibilities that it's better to get him to express his real concerns before you try to convince him of the advantages of owning versus renting.

Your first step in leading him to resolution is to say, *"It is a big step, but it's a step that very few people regret once they've done it. What is it about buying a home that concerns you?"* In this response, you have taken a small step to provide reassurance up front, but you have also left the door open for the customer to express his concerns so you can address them together as a team.

Whenever we are confused, concerned or afraid, verbalizing our feelings makes them more manageable. Remember that resolving customers' concerns is not about winning a debate, it's about achieving understanding, and helping them make a confident decision without buyer's remorse later.

Remember, too, as we discussed in Chapter Two, urgency may take time to develop, so don't be discouraged if it's not there at first. Even when a customer starts out rude, think to yourself, "Fifteen minutes from now they'll like me. I love turning customers like this around."

After learning about your customers, your next objective is not to create urgency, but to create interest in your homes and lead them to choose a favorite.

If customers seem discouraged by the prospects of getting what they want, you can take this approach: *"Let's put our heads together and explore the possibilities, and see if we can figure out a way to get you where you want to go."* This is one more way to create a sense of "shared purpose" with your customers.

If their first response indicates you probably don't have what they're looking for, use that as a springboard. *"It sounds as though what we have is different than what you're looking for. But as long as you're here, I'd be happy to tell you about what we are offering and why it has been so successful."* One reason you can always have hope, even when customers seem to want something you don't have, is this: **People start out with a plan and then change their plan when they find the home they want.**

What about the homes themselves? How much detail should you get into about the homes during the greeting stage of the sale? We have discussed the selling message, during which you summarize the highlights of your homes on a conceptual level. But what about the specifics? For our purposes here, we're going to hold off until our next chapter on demonstration to talk about this, even though part of it may begin in the sales office. At this point we're going to move to the last part of the greeting, which is to create a transition from the greeting to the demonstration stage of the sale.

Set Up the Next Stage of the Sale

The most important goal of each stage of the sale is to set up the next stage. This is how you sustain momentum in the selling process. As you wind down the greeting portion of the sale, you are ready to move on to the demonstration stage.

A vital part of selling is *creating transitions* from one stage of the sale to the next. Smaller transitions can make a difference, too – transitions from one moment of the sale to the next, especially to get past those moments when the momentum of a sale can suddenly fizzle. One example would be the awkward moments of silence that can be so pivotal in whether a sale stalls or keeps moving forward.

Then there is the transition moment when the stage of a sale is completed, such as the model tour or the trip to the site. These moments provide the perfect opportunity for a customer to say, "Thanks, we have someplace else we need to be, but you've sure given us a lot to think about." You need to develop a mental reflex for such moments that makes you say, "Keep it going."

How do you create this mental reflex? One way is through a mental image. For instance, imagine you are driving a car and the engine begins to stall. Do you hit the brake or the accelerator? The accelerator, of course. And yet in sales we may have a tendency to hit the brake with a comment such as, "So, do you have any other questions?" Another example would be to imagine that the selling process has a series of canyons where you need a bridge or you'll fall in. As the salesperson, you are the bridge builder. Don't let yourself, or the customer, fall into the canyon.

Whether you call it an accelerator or a bridge, what you need in order to keep the sale moving is a *transition*, and the easiest way to create a transition is through a *transition line*. Examples of transition lines would be:

- *"The next thing we need to talk about is…"*
- *"The next thing I need to show you is…"*
- *"The next thing I need to tell you about is…"*
- *"Another question many people ask is…"*
- *"Now that you've decided _____, the next thing you need to consider is…"*

In making the transition from the sales office to the model demonstration, your transition line could be as simple as, *"Let me show you our model,"* or, *"Let me show you what we have here."* Some salespeople prefer to use a point they are making in their overview as a springboard for their demonstration. For example, *"A lot of people are surprised by some of the things we include as standard features in our base price. Let me give you a few examples in our model."* Or, *"One thing we're known for is our architecture. Let me show you what I mean."*

A number of salespeople keep their brochures in the kitchen instead of the sales office. They present their overview in the sales office without a brochure, and then include the brochure and the guest card in their demonstration. *"I have some brochures in the kitchen. I'll get you started in the model and give you a brochure there."*

Naturally, your transition will be influenced by where you first greet your customers. It will be different if your office is in one of the rooms of the model home as opposed to the garage or an adjacent trailer.

You want to stay with the customer as long as it continues to be productive in order to create a seamless experience. You enrich that experience by building on points you made in your initial overview, and then by getting feedback as you go. There will be times when you feel as though the customer needs some space in order to get their bearings. In that case you could let them go alone for awhile, and then catch up with them after a few minutes.

Remember, your goal is momentum. You are always trying to get the customer to want to do one more thing, to go one step farther. Also remember the baseball diamond. You've hit your single (you've learned their situation and presented your selling message). Now it's time to go for second (pick out a favorite home). We'll see you there in our next chapter.

Conclusion

Using our baseball diamond analogy to represent the selling process, you have hit a single when you have learned the customer's situation and conveyed your selling message. The greeting stage of the sale – from the time a customer walks in your door until the time you begin your product demonstration (whether from blueprints, models, inventory homes or lots) – includes four goals that relate to hitting your single.

1. Begin building a relationship with customers.
2. Learn their needs, priorities, motivations, and initial level of urgency.
3. Determine their qualifications.

4. Give an overview of what you are selling, including your selling message.

* * *

From now on the exercises in the Conclusion of each chapter will focus on your preparation for each stage of the sale. Preparation takes time, but it is time well spent. It enables you to perform at your highest level every time. It also helps you create momentum; you always know what's coming next, so you can keep advancing the sale smoothly and confidently. Preparation improves your consistency, your confidence, and your ability to lead the sale.

The following exercises will help you bring together the basics and the magic of the greeting stage in order to engage your customers as much and as quickly as possible.

1. Create your Plan A (see page 47) in a way that covers the basics of the greeting in your own unique selling style. Plan A includes awareness of how you will be perceived by your customers when they first meet you, how you will break the ice, and what questions you will ask to begin forming a relationship.

    You should write out your Plan A in the form of a script, even if you wind up varying from your script in order to adapt to different situations.

2. Make a list of the other important questions you want to ask before you make your transition to the demonstration stage. These questions are designed to determine:
    - The customer's initial motivation – its source and its level
    - Their priorities and primary needs
    - Their ability to buy

3. Next create your Plan B, including your Brief Initial Overview (BIO) and your selling message. Once again, it is worth the time to write out this information so you can deliver it consistently, concisely, and with high impact. In addition to your selling message, write out the highlights that every customer needs to appreciate concerning your:

   - Location
   - Community
   - Homes
   - Home sites
   - Builder

4. Make a list of ten reasons why customers should buy a home at your community. Continue to update this list over time. You may find it helpful to ask past purchasers why they chose you.

5. What steps can you take in your own unique way, generally or specifically, to appeal to the "intuitive" element of the customers' decision process – to inspire feelings that they have found the place where everything feels right?

6. Make a list of the most frequent and challenging concerns that customers express at the beginning of the sale. Then write down ways you can probe further into their thoughts and feelings in order to help them address each challenge on their own terms.

7. Think of a few times when a previous interaction which looked promising suddenly stalled. Next, think of a transition line that could have kept it going.

Now it's time to make our own transition in the selling process, from the greeting stage to the demonstration stage.

The Basics and the Magic

CHAPTER

SHOWING YOUR HOMES AND SITES

The demonstration stage of the sale is a great opportunity to display the magic of selling. But the magic works hand in hand with the basics; the art of selling alone won't work without the science.

The sales office – the greeting stage – sets up the action. It's like the warmup stage of the sale. The homes and sites are where the real game is played. The emotional part of buying a home blossoms here. Everything you introduced conceptually in the greeting stage now comes to life. The appetizer is finished and the main course is now being served. Invite your customers to enjoy the finest meal they've ever had.

Unfortunately, this wonderful selling opportunity can slip away if the customer has to go through the model alone. Sometimes they are sent to the site alone, perhaps with a map or a borrowed set of keys to inventory homes. Perhaps the salesperson is afraid of annoying the customer by accompanying them, or he may believe he can be more productive doing something else. To be fair, both of these ideas are occasionally correct. If you are 100% sure that 1) the visitor will never be a potential purchaser, or 2) your chances of selling them a home will actually increase if you leave them alone, or 3) performing some other activity will be more likely to sell a home, then let the customer go alone.

However, in a series of focus groups with buyers who had closed on new homes within the previous six months (meaning that they had all made a buying decision and their buying experience was still vivid in their memory), the participants were asked to describe things about salespeople that had disappointed them. The three complaints that were voiced most often about new home salespeople in general were:

- Very few salespeople wanted to personally show me what they were trying to sell me.
- Very few salespeople asked me to buy what they were trying to sell me.
- Very few salespeople cared enough about me to follow up.

The respondents frequently explained that the salesperson from whom they bought was an exception to these generalizations.

This is an interesting twist on the "customers-don't-want-to-be-hassled" theory. Of course, the results would probably have been different if the focus groups were comprised of people who had not bought homes. Perhaps non-buyers would prefer to be left alone. But that raises an important issue. Buyers have different expectations than non-buyers, and it is the expectations of buyers we are trying to fulfill. It is better to offer our best service to a non-buyer and be told "no thanks" than to neglect a buyer for fear of intruding upon their space. If a visitor does not want diligent service they will let you know, and you can honor their request.

However, a first rate demonstration of homes and sites is one of the primary basics of selling, and the magic you add can engage customers in ways that touring alone can never achieve. In a moment we'll see how this happens. But first there's one more piece of business to attend to.

The Importance of Conversion Rate

The term "conversion rate" does not always inspire enthusiasm. (Its other name is "closing ratio" – the ratio of sales to traffic.) For some it conjures up fears of inadequacy, pressure and micromanagement. Please, please don't think of it that way. Think of conversion rate as a friend, not an enemy. Look at it like this: If you are currently closing one customer out of every twenty who visit your sales office, and you could figure out a skill, strategy or attitude that would enable you to close just one of the other nineteen, you would double your income. It's one of the marvels of our profession. There are very few careers where you can double your income so quickly. So don't think of conversion rate as a threatening vehicle of scrutiny from management. Think of it as one of your most powerful sales tools, and as the fastest, easiest way to give yourself a pay raise.

Remember that you don't just *make* sales, you also *win* them. You want to find every competitive advantage possible, and focusing on your conversion rate can lead you to a few more.

To increase your conversion rate, first remember the five demeanors customers want to see in a salesperson: confidence, enthusiasm, joy, relaxation and purpose. These demeanors will help you take a huge step toward converting one of the other nineteen.

Next, define what you believe is a selling opportunity. Is it a customer who expresses immediate enthusiasm for your homes? Is it someone who is respectful, or who engages willingly in conversation, or who asks you to show them your model and available home sites? Not necessarily. In order to maximize your selling opportunities and increase your conversion rate, you should define a selling opportunity as *anyone who has the ability to buy one of your homes (in terms of their finances and their basic requirements), regardless of their initial demeanor.*

What about buying signals? Again, is it enthusiasm? Again, not necessarily. **The most reliable buying signal is the willingness to make decisions.** If you have a buyer who has the ability to buy your homes, and who is willing to engage in decisions rather than deflecting them, this is a buyer you want to take as far as you can before letting the sale stop. We won't talk any more about buying signals here, but we'll revisit it in our chapters on objections and closing. For our purposes here in defining selling opportunities, just remember to keep an eye on the customer's behavior pattern regarding decisions.

The next step for increasing your conversion rate is to remember your baseball diamond. With every selling opportunity your goal is to get a triple (pick out a favorite site as well as a favorite home). While your ideal is always to make a complete sale, there are reasons that may not be possible, even with a viable selling opportunity. Nevertheless, assume there is no reason why you can't hit a triple on the first day. Even if you turn out to be wrong, you will still maximize your opportunity by assuming the triple is possible. Once you reach third base, then you can begin focusing on the final close.

Remember, don't be the one who stops the sale. Always get the customer to want to go one step farther. Create positive anticipation for the next stage, and build the bridge to get there.

Give yourself a pay raise by increasing your conversion rate. Increase your conversion rate – and provide better service to your customers – by maximizing each stage of the selling process.

Now let's get back to the model demonstration – how to use it to engage your customers and achieve the greatest selling impact.

Demonstrating Your Model

The term "show time" can evoke two kinds of responses. It can evoke an enthusiastic response from salespeople who see it as the art of selling, or a negative response from those who think it dehumanizes selling by making it seem shallow and contrived. Think of "show time" in the positive sense of providing the best possible experience for the customer. Great selling relies partly on a passion for the artistic element. Like any artist, you offer enrichment. You help your customers experience your homes at a richer, more profound level. How do you provide a richer experience than anyone else the customer will visit?

It Begins With the Right Preparation

Great performances are sometimes described as "magical." Special moments in your life may have seemed magical as well. Great performers provide magical moments for their audiences. Great salespeople do the same. You want every customer who visits you to say, "That person (or place) was really special. I want to go back. I want to live in that home and in that place. I want to buy my home from that person." How do you inspire those feelings in your customers? How do you provide magical moments?

A brilliant demonstration is a magnificent work of art. As in the performing arts, providing a magical experience in our profession requires preparation, and in new home sales you are not only the performer, you are also the writer. You create your performance at both levels. Just as writers produce drafts, painters produce sketches and sculptors produce models, you will need to create your script and then continue to refine it. Just as actors and singers rehearse and practice, so, too, you will practice to enrich your performance. Your demonstration is your masterpiece. Salespeople who do not commit this much effort to their masterpiece will lose more sales to you than they win from you.

Preparation will not only increase the impact of your demonstration, it will also enhance your position as the leader in the relationship. This will help you maintain control of the sale. It will also increase your customers' trust and confidence in you.

Don't think of repetition as tedious. While you will deliver your presentation many times, each customer will only experience it once. You want every demonstration to be as powerful as your best one.

Your rehearsal should include:

- The sequence of your demonstration, room by room

- The points you will make, and the words you will use to make them
- The questions you will ask to elicit responses and decisions (These last two items will require a tape recorder, so you can play back your words to see how your voice inflections sound.)
- The facial expressions and body language you will use (This will require a mirror.)

With these exercises you are practicing your style as well as your content. In addition to practicing by yourself, practice with a partner – another salesperson, an assistant, a spouse or a friend. Ask how they respond to your demonstration as they imagine themselves in the role of the customer.

The sources of magic in your presentation include:

- The personality you display
- The enthusiasm you show for your homes, community, location, builder, and, most of all, for your customers
- The way you bring the special benefits of your homes to life
- Showing customers that they are the center of your world, and that you are interested in who they are, what they think, and what they want
- Your interest in helping them to fulfill their mission (instilling a sense of shared purpose for finding solutions to their problems)
- The questions you ask to help them choose the right home (This includes using the model as a springboard for the other homes that are available.)
- The guidance you provide by using their responses to give them direction

All of these items are part of the screenplay you are writing and rehearsing. This may sound like a lot of work, but you should be able to complete it in a day or two, and the benefits of this exercise will enhance your success for the rest of your career. The time and effort you commit to preparing and practicing each stage of your sales presentation will be one of your most rewarding career investments.

Now that we have talked about *how* to prepare, let's discuss *what* to prepare. We'll begin at the beginning, stepping back for a moment into the sales office where you set up the transition to the model demonstration.

Getting the Model Demonstration Started

When you make the transition from the sales office to the model, you are also making the transition from selling ideas to selling homes. Your primary goal in showing a model is to help customers decide which of your homes is best for them. You are not trying to sell them the model. You are using your model to represent your builder and your entire line of homes, including what makes your homes special in the marketplace. Your model becomes the springboard for choosing which of your floor plans to focus on.

You want the transition from sales office to model to be smooth, and you also want it to propel the sale forward. In our last chapter, we discussed transitioning from the sales office to the model home in a way that is comfortable for both you and the customer. Of course, if your sales office is in the home itself, and the customer always enters by the front door, the transition is simpler. If you have no models (as with a preopening trailer or a small community where you sell the entire community without models), then all of your transitions occur in one place, and your demonstration consists of creating a vision from floor plans and site plans. Our focus in this chapter will be limited to a situation where your sales office is in a garage (or a trailer adjacent to a model), and where you only have one model to show.

Occasionally a customer can clearly explain the kind of home they want so you can begin the decision process before seeing a model, then zero in on one or two house types using sales office displays, blueprints, or floor plans from your brochure. If they are willing to focus on specific floor plans in depth, try to get them to a desk or table so they can focus more effectively in a relaxed seated position. You might even determine which house type is their favorite. In that case you could skip the model demonstration altogether and go to a field home of that type, if one is available.

If you do not have a field home, use the model as a frame of reference for the home of their choice. Show what features you include as standard, what options are available, and what features make your homes a better value than other homes in your market. You can use the rooms in your model to describe corresponding rooms in the home you are discussing, even if the rooms in your model are different. If you are showing features of your model and relating them to the floor plan of the other home from the brochure, it still makes the other home easier to envision.

Whether you are making the transition from the sales office to the model, or from the model to another home, make sure you prepare in advance how you will make these transitions, so you will be comfortable when the moment arrives. Examples of "transition lines" from the sales office to the model are as follows:

- *"Let me show you one of our homes."*
- *"Let me show you our model."*
- *"Let's have a look at an example of what we offer, and I'll point out a few standard and custom features as we go."*
- *"I have some brochures in the kitchen. Let's go get one, and I'll get you started."*
- *"Let me show you this home, and that will give me a chance to tell you a little more about us as a company, and how we do things. Also, as we're walking through, if you could tell me things you like and don't like, it will help us figure out if we have a home that might interest you."*

Go outside so you enter the model through the front door. That will give you a chance to talk about your company's approach to architecture, and how important the overall aesthetics of the community are to your company. Some salespeople make the mistake of believing that the home purchase is primarily about the floor plan, but research into consumer preferences proves otherwise. The look of a home is important to customers. This is because while the floor plan relates to the function of a home, the exterior relates to pride of ownership. Be sure to use the word "architecture" as opposed to merely "exterior" or "elevation." Surprisingly, the word "architecture" is rarely used in our industry for the outside or the inside, but it's a word that customers appreciate. Point out details that make your architecture special, and find out if your customers have any immediate preferences for exterior architecture.

Getting the Demonstration into Full Swing

Now you're inside the home, and the artistic part of your selling style reaches its full fruition. Have fun with this part of the sale. You owe that to yourself, and it will make the experience special for your customers as well.

Let your customers see the artistic work in your product. Help them to appreciate the work of the other artists involved – those who put their talents into designing, packaging, building and merchandising your model home. Help them appreciate the thought and care that went into designing and building each of your homes. Point out things that make your homes different – special – better. Include several construction techniques in your demonstration, as well as architectural features, standard features, and custom (optional) features. Point out features and benefits that are important advantages of your homes, especially ones that customers would not appreciate on their own.

Enthusiasm can be expressed powerfully by any kind of personality – from quiet to flamboyant, from analytical to emotional. You love your homes, you love showing them, and you love selling them. Enjoy whatever gifts of personality you possess. Let those gifts blossom through your smile, your eye contact, your voice, your motions, your energy, and your sincere interest in what your customer thinks, how they respond, what they want – what it is that will enrich and improve their lives.

Get Feedback As You Go

Keep your communication interactive. While you have prepared the points you want to highlight during your demonstration, also be sure to highlight features that relate to

The Basics and the Magic

preferences your customers have already stated. Keep asking for feedback as you continue through the demonstration. Carry a brochure with you as you tour the model so you can switch gears quickly and begin talking about other homes as needed.

The customer's feedback, and your use of it, keep the sale moving forward, and keep the decision-making rhythm building. Ask what parts of the home are most important to them, and focus your demonstration accordingly. Here are examples of other questions you can ask to get feedback and decisions as you go:

- *"How does this look to you?"*
- *"How do you like this home so far?"*
- *"Do you feel good about this?*
- *"Does this look like what you were talking about?"*
- *"How does this compare with what you were hoping for?"*
- *"How does this compare with other homes you've seen?"*
- *"How does this compare with your present home?"*
- [If there is another decision-maker who is not present, ask:] *"How do you think he/she will like it?"*
- *"How do you feel about this kitchen? Will it work for you?"*
- *"What is your favorite part of this home?"*
- *"How does this compare with the last one we looked at?"*
- *"Which one do you like best so far? What makes it your favorite?"*
- *"Is this a possibility for you?"*
- *"Is there anything about this home that doesn't work for you?"*

As you get answers to your questions and reactions to your homes, be sure to respond to their responses. Your customers must see that their responses are important to you. Responding with interest and enthusiasm to their feedback will encourage customers to communicate more.

Bring Your Selling Message to Life

Remembering your baseball diamond will help you develop momentum in your selling process. It is also how you give yourself a pay raise by increasing your conversion rate. Just keep going from one base to the next.

You hit a single in your greeting by learning the customer's situation and conveying your selling message. Your selling message is a concept. The model is where you begin to bring that concept to life and give examples that prove it, so that the concept becomes real in the mind and eyes of the customer. During the greeting stage, your BIO (Brief Initial Overview) is where you say, "Here are some of the reasons people choose our homes." The model demonstration is where you say, "Let me show you what I mean." Your selling message sets up your model demonstration; your demonstration brings the selling message to life.

As you plan and rehearse your model demonstration, choose several features you believe will have the most impact and significance for your buyer. Pay special attention to any information your customer provides regarding features that are important to them, but resort back to your original plan if they have not yet offered any helpful information.

The model demonstration is a great place to give examples of what makes your builder special, as well as your homes, and to explain how your company has achieved its success and reputation.

Create a Sense of Anticipation for the Home Sites You Are About to Show

You have hit a double when your customers decide which home is best for them. Now you are rounding second and heading for third. You hit a triple when customers pick out a favorite site to go with their favorite home. If they are looking for a quick move-in home, then you are going to the home and the lot at the same time. If they are looking for a to-be-built home, then you will be leading them to choose a home site from among those that are available.

The objective of every stage of the sale is not only to get a decision, but also to get to the next stage of the sale. **Always get the customer to want to do one more thing.** In the sales office you can begin to create anticipation for the home sites while standing at the site plan. In the model, you can look out the windows at examples of the kinds of lots that are available. Or you can simply describe them. As with the transition from the sales office to the model, you want to move them to the next stage as seamlessly as possible. If you have already discussed a particular site, then the transition is simple: *"Let's have a look at that site."* In case you don't have this opportunity, prepare a generic approach you would use for such occasions. An example would be: *"The next thing I'd like to do is show you where these homes (home sites) are located. While we're looking at them, you can also get a better idea of what the neighborhood is (will be) like."*

Going to the Site

On your baseball diamond, you're heading for third. The sale is becoming visible. It's getting exciting, and the magic keeps getting better. And what a great setting for magic to occur! You're moving from the indoor adventure to the outdoor adventure.

The trip to the site is the most adventurous part of the sale. You are walking through the community, describing what a wonderful place it is for the people who live there, what a wonderful place it is for you to work, how much you've enjoyed selling to your homeowners, how much they enjoy their home and their neighborhood, and how much your new customer will enjoy living there.

You also get to create a vision for what is yet to come – in the community as a whole and on the particular site you are showing.

But wait a minute. What if there is nothing exciting about the individual site you are showing? What if it's only average? What if all your lots are only average? Where's the adventure – the excitement – the emotional selling – the one-of-a-kind urgency – the magic? Maybe this is why the lot-showing stage – the stage that sets up the close – is so underestimated and underutilized, and why so many sales lose their momentum here. Maybe it's because we don't get excited enough about most of the home sites we're trying to sell. After all, where's the hope for creating excitement and urgency for any lot other than the best one we have? And what if that best one is only average by the standards of the market? Or what if it has a huge premium?

There are two places in the selling process where many salespeople are too easily discouraged. As we have already discussed, the first is at the beginning when customers do not seem eager to establish rapport. The second discouragement is over challenging lots.

How do we get more excited about mediocre lots? By realizing *that's what the overwhelming majority of people buy*. Why? Because they buy the total package. Help your customers to see the total quality of life that only your home and community can provide.

It is interesting to see the way different salespeople are better at selling different kinds of lots – large or small, flat or sloping, corner lots, or lots backing to roads or power lines. When selling a variety of lot conditions, attitude is as important as experience.

Have you ever caught yourself saying, "What in the world does he see in her?" or, "How could she have married him?" or, "That guy doesn't deserve a friend as good as George." In each case you see one person who finds what they want in another. They look at the person in a special way because different things are important to them. They see good traits in the person so clearly that they overlook flaws that someone else would consider unacceptable. This is the kind of unconditional love you need to have for each and every site you offer. At work, your home sites are your children, and you have to love each one in its own special way. So the first person you have to sell is yourself. Walk your sites until you figure out how to love each one enough to sell it with confidence, enthusiasm, joy, purpose and relaxation. Then you will have discovered one more dimension in the magic of selling.

Now let's review.

Your primary purposes in taking customers to see your home sites are to:

1. Sell the community with greater impact than you could in the sales office.
2. Engage customers in one particular home site (get them to choose a favorite).
3. Set up the close.

A couple of principles we discussed for demonstrating your model apply similarly to showing home sites.

Your best opportunity to give yourself a pay raise is by increasing your conversion rate. Don't wonder if your customers want you to accompany them. If there is any question, it is better to err on the side of good service. Serious buyers expect attentive service. They want to be taken seriously, and are disappointed when they are just turned loose to sell themselves a home. Those rare occasions when you would send a customer to the site alone (you are 100% sure they are not in the market, but they're curious anyway; they want to learn more about the community where their friend or relative bought; or you have an appointment with a serious prospect five minutes from now) become a judgment call based solely on your desire to maximize every opportunity.

Prepare your process of showing sites just as you prepare your model demonstration. Again, you are the artist. You are creating and performing another part of the presentation that provides a more enriching experience at your community than they will receive any place else they visit. Let them see that you love what you do.

You are going for a triple – the customers choose their favorite site. Your best chance of getting customers to choose one is by collaborating with them each step of the way. Help them to experience the sites from your point of view. Keep the experience interactive. Ask questions, get feedback, and adjust your selling strategy to their feedback as you go. Don't be the one who stops the sale.

Now let's discuss some specific skills for showing sites, leading the decision, and setting up the close. Included will be some information adapted from *Success in New Home Sales* and *Selling with Momentum* by Rich Tiller.

Creating a Vision at the Site

What do we mean when we talk about "helping the customer to create a vision of their new home?" It means much more than simply taking a customer to a site and saying, "Imagine yourself living here someday." It involves a combination of artistic and technical skills.

Suppose you are taking a customer to a home site on which construction has not yet started and even the grading is not completed. The tools you need with you are a site plan (or engineering plan), an engineer's ruler and a 100-foot tape. Standing on the site, you explain how the lot will slope, how drainage will work, where and how the home will be sited. Don't just walk up to the lot, walk on to it, all the way to the back. Walking on the site is the first tangible step toward ownership. It takes the adventure to the next level. Keep the prospect involved by such means as having him or her to hold one end of the tape, or stand at one of the lot corners while you demonstrate its size. This is the technical aspect of creating a vision. It adds substance, credibility and understanding to the vision.

You exercise your artistic expertise as you verbally paint your picture, using whatever visual props you have at your disposal: the brochure, site plan, or other homes nearby. Look for features or benefits that may become elements in your vision, such as views; trees; future landscaping; home siting relative to the sun; access to community features; home features which may also relate to the lot (sunroom, deck, windows, etc.); lot size, usable space, and lot aesthetics; privacy; maintenance benefits; great neighbors. Ask your builder, or someone from your land department who has worked with your site plan, to walk the lots with you and offer their perspective on each site.

You can use your 100-foot tape to explain future grading. Walk the appropriate distance to make the scale of the grade change accurate, and then move your end of the tape up to the height of the grade change. It is also impressive if you can train yourself to take a pace of exactly two feet or three feet, so you don't have to use the tape every time.

Even if construction has not started on the home, you can create involvement by "walking through the home" on the vacant site using house plans. This will help customers understand the views from each of the rooms, and the effect of sunlight during different times of the day. If there is a grade change to the home behind you, explain how it will provide a sense of separation or privacy more than looking out one rear window directly into another one.

Relate your verbal painting to needs the customer has already expressed and to the competitive advantages you have over other homes the customer may be considering. Without this focus, the most eloquently expressed vision may not necessarily create customer involvement or urgency. Give credibility to your vision with examples of how it appeals to others, or to you personally. Here is an example for a home site that slopes up in the back.

"You mentioned you wanted more privacy than with a typical site, but you don't want to pay a premium. That made me think of this site for you. There is enough flat space to install your swing, and then the lot slopes up to the home behind you giving you a better sense of separation. Instead of looking out your rear window into another home, you're looking at your grassy slope. If you landscape the slope, it creates a nicer setting than you ever get with a flat lot. That's why a lot of folks prefer a home site like this – it gives you better aesthetics and more of a sense of privacy without paying extra for it. In addition, the home faces north/south so you'll have sun in your front and back yards all day."

Remember that you not only create a vision for living in the home on the site, you also create a vision for living in the neighborhood. Look for opportunities any time during the sale, including your trip to the sites, to enhance your vision with anecdotes about other people who have bought your homes. These anecdotes have an impact that other forms of information cannot have, because customers relate to anecdotes on a more human level. The same principle applies to third-party endorsements that you can pass on from previous buyers. For example:

"The family four doors up also bought the Franklin model, and they love it. They hit the walking trails together three evenings a week and walk around the pond. They say it's the per-

fect way to end their day. They also say the road behind them doesn't bother them at all, and that they'd rather have the road than another home. If you'd like, I can introduce you to them. I think you'll really like them. We have lots of great neighbors here."

Showing Homes That Are Under Construction

If you are showing a home already under construction, consider that seeing a home under construction is another adventure that enriches the buying experience for customers. It is also an experience they will not always get, because many salespeople try to sidestep that part of the sale. Perhaps they don't feel comfortable with their construction knowledge. Sometimes they just don't enjoy going to homes under construction themselves. Or possibly they think the experience will be difficult for their customers. On the contrary, seeing a home under construction helps to create involvement if the experience is led by a skilled salesperson.

It is important not to appear self-conscious about showing homes during various stages of construction. Customers need to see that you are comfortable selling homes this way. It will make them more comfortable knowing that people buy homes this way. Don't apologize or say, "I know it's going to be difficult to imagine what this home will look like when it's finished." You are the expert. If you say it's difficult to view a home under construction, then it's difficult. If you say it's easy, then it's easy.

Take them through a home under construction as you would a finished home. Be sure you take a floor plan with you. You may need to give a little more explanation of the rooms to help orient the customer, but otherwise sell the basic features and benefits as though you were in a model. Ask for feedback from customers periodically to make sure they can visualize what you are showing them. Usually they can, but if they are having trouble, then you know you must devote a little more time to explanation. For most customers, the experience of walking through a home that is only in framing grows on them as they progress, and it becomes easier for them to understand as they become more comfortable with it.

Explain as simply as possible what a room will look like when it's finished. Then ask, *"Are you picturing this okay?"* Also ask customers what they think from time to time to be sure they are relating to the home and progressing through the decision process. Tell why other people have liked particular features, and why you like them, too. This is another way to "bring the home to life."

Selecting the Favorite Home Site

One of the inherent characteristics of every piece of real estate is its uniqueness. Like snowflakes and fingerprints, no two are exactly the same. No matter how similar your home sites may be, there is always one which will suit your customer best. Once the customer has decided which site is their favorite, make sure you understand why. If you're not already sure, ask them. You need to know, and their conviction will be even stronger once they express it.

As soon as they pick their favorite, the potential for fear of loss comes into play, and this becomes one more source of urgency. It is reasonable for them to believe that the next customer who walks in will feel the same way about the same site. This leaves your current customer with the choice of making a decision now, or possibly settling for their second choice later because someone else was more decisive. Some salespeople ask their customers to pick a second choice for just this purpose. Of course, this kind of urgency and fear of loss can't kick in until customers have decided they want the home and site.

You may need to help them make their decision. If such help is needed, don't feel shy about giving it. After all, you're the expert. You may have to go out on a limb by suggesting which of your sites you feel will be best for them. This is one way to create a sense of interest, or positive anticipation, for customers who visit your home sites. Your suggestion is based on information they have already given you regarding their preferences. If they have not provided such information, you can take your best shot based on your own judgment, and let them agree or disagree. If they disagree and prefer a different site, there is no harm done. You do not have to defend your position. You have still helped them to make a decision.

Setting Up the Close

Once a customer picks a favorite home site, you have rounded third base and are heading for home. This is no time to slow down; it's time to pick up speed. The sale is in clear view.

For many salespeople, the site is their favorite closing venue. They go for the close in the simplest way possible. *"Do you like this home (site)?...Would you like to have it?"*

If something doesn't seem quite right, a more gradual

approach might be better. At this point you have to rely on your gut.

- *"How does all this look (feel) to you?"*
- *"Is this coming together for you?"*
- *"Are we making good progress?"*
- *"Do you have a good feeling about this?"*
- *"How are you feeling about the whole idea of moving?"*
- *"How do you like this compared to where you live now?"* (*"Do you feel as though life will be better here than where you live now?"*)

Regarding this last question, remember that your fiercest competitor is often your customer's current home. You must not allow your customers to slip back into complacency once they have expressed the desire to move. (Remember one of your first questions from the greeting stage: *"What is it that's gotten you thinking about moving?"*) You are a doctor whose job is to locate the pain which caused the customer to seek a doctor in the first place. You must then prescribe the appropriate cure. Sometimes the patient decides to forego the cure and go on living with the pain. The doctor's job is to remind the patient that if pain goes untreated, it is likely to get worse. The doctor may even have to poke at the painful spot to remind the patient of the importance of taking constructive action.

Like the doctor, the new home salesperson devotes his or her career to relieving pain – "quality of life pain." You must sell the patient on the fact that your treatment is better than his pain, and that his pain will only grow more difficult and costly to cure as time goes on. In buying a new home, as in curing an ailment, procrastination can often make the solution much more difficult to achieve.

In medicine, this process is called treatment. In new home sales, it is called closing.

For those who prefer not to close at the site, there are other options. Once a favorite site has been selected, some salespeople prefer to return to the sales office, discuss financing, and then ask for the sale. In this approach it can still be helpful to present the buying scenario at the site – before you reach the closing stage of the sale – so when the closing situation does arrive it is more familiar. An example of this strategy would be to say, *"When folks decide to buy a home here, what we do is write up a purchase agreement which includes a deposit of $_____. The rest is due when you move in."* With this approach you not only prepare them for the close which is coming, you also get an opportunity to test their initial reaction to this information without requiring a commitment.

We will pick up the topic of closing in our final chapter. First, we will take a detour into the world of objections.

Conclusion

In order to create magic in your selling, you must connect with your customers in a special way. Showing your models, homes under construction and home sites to customers is one of the best ways to expand and deepen those connections. You connect with customers by:

- Enjoying them
- Being interested in them

- Understanding their needs, motivations and ability to buy
- Earning their trust
- Locking into their mission of improving their lives by helping them decide which of your homes is best

A demonstration is not something you do to a customer, but an experience you share with them. The magic of demonstration comes easily when you're happy to see a customer because you can't wait to show them what you have. You are helping customers to catch your contagious enthusiasm for your homes, your community and your company. You provide the experience, they provide the responses, and then you use their responses to tailor the experience to fulfill their needs.

Creating the ultimate experience for your customers requires preparation and practice. Write down exactly what you want to accomplish in demonstrating not only your model, but also your homes and sites in the field. It takes time, but the time is well worth it, because it will take your demonstrations to a higher level, increase your conversion rate, and pay you handsomely for the time you invest in preparation.

As in giving speeches, some people work better from a complete script, while others work better from an outline. Use whichever one you prefer. Practice it until you believe your customers will be positively influenced by it. As you prepare your script or outline, include the following:

- *A transition line from your sales office to the model, and from the model to the field.*
- *The room sequence you will follow in showing your*

models. You can adapt this sequence if you believe it will benefit a particular customer, based on information they give you. However, you should start out with a plan, so you can provide leadership and consistency.
- *A general concept of the order in which you will show homes and home sites in the field.* For example, how many will you show? Will you save the best for last, or will you take your best shot first? Each school of thought has its followers, so make sure you know where you stand so you can lead the customer with confidence and purpose.
- *Several highlights you will point out in your model.* Include exterior features as well as interior ones. These highlights can relate to features that:
  a. Demonstrate your basic selling message
  b. Give you an advantage over the competition
  c. Provide benefits that customers would not see or appreciate by themselves
  d. The customers said were important to them (Of course, you will decide these on the spot, since you will not know them in advance.)
- *How you will create a sense of positive anticipation for visiting your home sites.*
- *Features that make each home site special.*
- *What you will do when you walk on to a home site with a customer.* This includes how you will show the site, and also how you will create a vision of the home on the site.
- *How you will show homes that are in various stages of construction.*
- *Answers to potential objections that may be raised to*

your homes or sites. Our next chapter will also help you in this area.
- *Questions you will ask along the way in order to elicit responses and decisions.* This would include "trial closes."
- *How you will use the trip to the home sites to set up the close.*

Prepare not only what you will say, but how you will say it. Always be aware of your "stage presence." It is an important part of the impact you will have and the connection you will make with your customers.

Chapter

HANDLING OBJECTIONS

Handling objections doesn't sound like a very magical topic, unless we can wave a magic wand and make them disappear. No, we can't do that, but then maybe we shouldn't want to. Maybe the magic in overcoming objections is not in making them disappear, but in using them to make a sale. Taking something that could prevent a sale and turning it around to make a sale – how cool is that?

Objections are a healthy and necessary part of the customer's decision making process. Raising an objection and then resolving it is part of the system of checks and balances that helps customers make decisions with greater confidence. Objections are one of the ways customers ask themselves, "Am I really sure about this?" But then when the answer is yes, it's a stronger decision than they would have made without addressing the question. Objections help customers make decisions they won't regret later. We need to see objections as a friend and not an enemy.

Wait a minute. Objections aren't always our friend. What if we can't overcome them? They could kill the sale. To solve this puzzle, let's begin by making a crucial distinction between *objections* and *conditions*.

Objections vs. Conditions

Objections are concerns for which a customer needs resolution or reassurance. Objections do not always have to be overcome. Sometimes an objection only needs to be accepted, because the customer likes everything else about the home well enough that they are convinced it is the best home for them, all things considered. They simply have to be willing to compromise. The customer needs your help in addressing these objections, either through resolution or through reassurance. How to fulfill this need will be the main topic of our chapter. But first, let's talk about conditions.

A condition is a requirement. It is beyond our control, and often beyond the customer's control as well. It is something that must be a certain way because of something else that cannot be changed. Here are a few examples of conditions:

- The customers absolutely cannot afford a home of more than $300,000 because of their income and the amount of cash they have for a down payment.
- They absolutely must have four bedrooms because of the size of their family, or because of specific uses for each room that cannot be accommodated any other way.
- They must have a one-level home because they are unable to climb stairs.
- They must have a flat yard to accommodate a pool for a child that is aspiring to become an Olympic swimmer.
- The home must have two master bedrooms because two couples will be sharing the home.

If your homes cannot meet these conditions, then it's not about overcoming objections. Those customers simply do not represent the market for your homes. They are not prospects. It's black and white. There's nothing wrong with you, there's nothing wrong with your homes, and there's nothing wrong with the customer.

An objection is when a customer says there is something about your home that is different than what they *want*, but is not impossible to accept. This is the battleground on which sales are won or lost. The customer wants a larger home site but doesn't actually need one. Or they want to back up to trees. Or they want larger bedrooms, or they don't want to back up to a road. They want four bedrooms, even though they only need three, because their "advisor" told them that a four-bedroom home is better for resale. Sales are won when customers want something, but are willing to let it go because something else about the home compels them to change their priorities. In other words, they become willing to compromise. This is where we get into the magic.

Now that we've distinguished between *conditions* that make a sale impossible and *objections* that need to be resolved, we're ready to go to the next step – how to handle those objections that really do make a difference.

Let Customers Talk It Through

When customers raise concerns, our first impulse is often to squash the problem before it gets out of control. Here's an example. In 2008, a lot of people raise questions about the market. A typical objection is, "I don't feel as though now is a good time to buy." The first question to ask yourself is, "Why is the customer saying that?" Did he drive all the way out to your community just to tell you that now is not a good time to buy, especially if he's never visited you before? Why would he do that? Maybe he's looking for someone to "give him permission" to buy in this tough market. It may be too soon for you to figure out what he's really up to. There's only one thing you know for sure – *he came to you*. If you had chased him down the street and wrestled him to the ground, and then asked for the sale, it would make sense for him to say, "I don't feel as though now is a good time to buy." But that's not what happened. So first you need to gain a better understanding of what's going on in the customer's mind.

As the expert, you are a counselor in areas where you have more knowledge than they do. Embrace that role with confidence and enthusiasm. Customers want to see our five favorite demeanors now as much as ever: confidence, enthusiasm, joy, purpose and relaxation. Don't panic over objections. Think of them as feedback, not obstacles. Objections are not like bugs that we have to stomp on before they bite. They are simply concerns that customers are trying to resolve. If they didn't want help resolving them, they wouldn't express them. They would just tell you they don't want your home and walk away.

Like a counselor, don't try to solve their problems for them instantly. Make sure you understand the issue and, more importantly, make sure they understand the issue. So often the problem is that customers haven't thought the issue all the way through. They have become victim to their own partial thoughts. Once we think an issue all the way through, and put our thoughts into words, the issue becomes more finite, more manageable, easier to understand, and easier to resolve.

If customers express concerns about the market, help them try to understand their concerns first, and then you will understand them better. Resist the temptation to jump right in and say, "Are you kidding? This is a great time to buy. Let me tell you why." Instead, ask them, *"How do you feel about buying a home in this market?"* Other follow up questions could include:

- *"What has brought you out looking in this market?"*
- *"What is your vision for being in the market right now? What would be the ideal ending to your journey?"*
- *"How will you know when the time is right?"*
- *"If you did find the perfect home, what would you do?"* (*"If you found a home that would really make you happy, what would be your next step?"*)
- *"How has your search been going so far?"*
- *"What is it that will make you say, 'My journey is over; my mission is complete'?"*

Another example would be if they say, "I want to know I'm getting the best deal in the market." Instead of jumping right into a debate, ask them, *"How will you know when you've gotten the best deal?"*

Once they have expressed their concern thoroughly enough that you both understand what they are trying to achieve, then you can start talking it through with them. The more they can participate in finding the right answer, the more they will believe in the answer they find. They need to be part of the solution just as much as you do. After all, the best connection you can establish with your customers is one of shared purpose in fulfilling their needs, resolving their questions and addressing their concerns.

How Important Is the Objection?

One challenge with objections is determining whether they are truly a factor in the customer's decision. Sometimes people raise objections just to make conversation or create a smoke screen, while other times they are expressing a real concern that needs to be resolved in order for them to keep moving forward.

If there is any doubt about what their concern might be, go ahead and ask, *"What is it that concerns you?"*

Then you need to know how important the objection really is, so you don't waste time and energy fighting battles that don't matter. When the objection is easy to resolve, go ahead and resolve it. However, if you cannot resolve the objection right away, use responses such as these to put the objection on hold until you understand what else is going on:

- *"How do you like the home other than that?"*
- *"How important is this? Is it a priority?"*
- *"Hold on to that thought, and let's see what you think of the rest of the home. Then we can talk some more about…[whatever the issue is that they brought up]."*

If the objection is a "deal killer," and there is nothing you can do to resolve it, then you need to know that. Sometimes an objection means, "I will not accept this home, no matter what you say."

Most of the time, if customers are seriously considering your home, an objection means they are sincerely questioning an issue and want to talk it through. They're saying, "I'm concerned about this. Tell me why I shouldn't be." They may like your home better than anything else they have seen, but need reassurance that they will be making the right decision by buying it. Or they may simply not yet have decided what they want, and need to put their questions on the table in the form of concerns or objections.

Don't Lose Hope – Customers Will Compromise

We said at the beginning of this chapter that part of the magic in handling objections is seeing the opportunity they provide for moving the sale forward – in fact, perhaps even achieving a breakthrough. Sometimes raising an objection is exactly what it takes for a customer to reach a buying decision. A customer who just says yes to everything may, in fact, be raising a red flag that they are not seriously engaged in making decisions. Sometimes customers will keep saying yes to humor you, or to postpone hurting your feelings, when, in fact, they're not really grappling with a decision at all. They know they will pull the plug before it's too late. Objections may be a customer's first genuine sign of interest – their first sincere buying signal. While they have created a hurdle, they are also willing to overcome the hurdle in order to get the home they really want. They just want to do it cautiously.

An interesting behavior pattern to watch for is whether the customers are trying to make the sale easier or harder – whether they are trying to move the sale forward, or keep it in neutral, or throw it into reverse. Watch the customers' behavior patterns regarding decisions, and consider the following questions:

- Are they trying to solve problems, or merely create them?
- Are they trying to make the sale happen, or keep it

from happening?
- Are they willing to participate in the solutions to their problems, or are they creating one problem after another just to put you through your paces without making any decisions or commitments in return?
- Are they trying to make a decision, even if they are struggling with it, or are they merely deflecting decisions?
- Are they trying to buy a home, or are they simply pretending?

If you are watching for these patterns in their behavior, you will find them where they exist. But if you're not watching, you can get sucked into "pretender syndrome."

Real buyers know that they will eventually have to compromise. No one gets everything they want when buying a home. Sacrifices and tradeoffs are a part of any major decision, and everyone knows it. People don't make major decisions by holding out for perfection. That's how people avoid decisions they don't want to make. People who make decisions choose from what's available in the real world, and it's all imperfect. People are willing to tolerate imperfections in things they really want. They are willing to accept what they don't want in order to get what they do want. Once a real buyer finds the best home for them in the real world – once they find the home that will most improve their lives for a price they can afford – they will accept its shortcomings. This is where the confidence and reassurance you provide through the connection you have created come to fruition.

An objection is *an unfavorable comparison in the customer's mind between your home and their ideal.* But when the time comes for them to make their final decision, their ideal will no longer be an option. They will have to decide which of the available choices will provide the best overall quality of life. No one else's home will match their ideal either, and their current home isn't matching it. At some point every customer compromises in order to justify their decision to buy the home they want the most.

How do you provide the magic that turns an objection into a decision?

Project the Right Demeanor

The magic of selling kicks in when objections draw you and your customers closer together instead of dividing you. Here your demeanor becomes critical. You are not their opponent in a debate. You are joining forces with them to resolve their issues. Too often we think of overcoming objections as a sparring match, a battle of wits – winner take all. Instead, use objections as a vehicle to advance your shared purpose of figuring out the best way to improve their lives. You are their counselor and their leader.

Show appreciation and respect for their objection. Act interested in it, and in helping them to find the resolution that is best for them. You are helping them to fulfill their mission. Consider these words: *"Let's put our heads together and figure out a way to get you where you want to go."* When they finally find an ally in their search for the right home, the magic comes to life. Your community becomes "the place where everything feels right."

When you are offering a solution, give it the tone of a brainstorming session as opposed to a lecture or debate. For example:

- *"Let me run an idea past you."*
- *"What do you think of this idea?"* Then provide your suggestion in the same tone you would when making a suggestion to your best friend.
- *"How would you feel about _____?"*

Help Customers Rethink Their Needs

The magic of selling also comes from balancing those needs a customer knows they have with those they don't yet realize. They start their home buying journey with an initial set of priorities, but then those priorities evolve as they begin to learn about the tradeoffs they will eventually have to make.

They also form their initial priorities in the vacuum of their imagination. They don't know what they don't know. One of the things they don't know is what you can give them that no one else can for your price. Your homes, sites, neighborhood, location and service program provide a combination that is unique in all the world, and is a combination they have never imagined. So while it is important to learn and honor a customer's needs and wants, it is equally important to remember that those needs and wants are a moving target. They are a work in progress, and they continue to evolve throughout the course of the customer's journey.

Sometimes fulfilling needs involves helping customers to rethink their needs, especially when they are raising objections to a home they are seriously interested in buying. Customers often wind up buying a home that is different from what they originally said they wanted, just as they wind up buying a home for thirty-day completion when they originally came in planning to buy "in about a year." **Customers start out with a plan, and then change their plan when they find the home they want.**

Your company designed your homes to fulfill certain needs that a portion of the market will have. Sometimes in order to fulfill a need, you must create the need in your customer's mind. In other words, make the customer aware that the need exists. They may realize that the need you are fulfilling will actually benefit them more than the need they originally wanted you to fulfill. You can begin to increase the customer's awareness of certain needs by showing how you have fulfilled the needs of others like them.

When customers raise an objection to your home, you can help them evolve their needs and broaden their horizons in two ways:

1. *Explain why your builder chose this approach.* Provide an explanation. Explain to your customers why your builder chose to do it this way, and why other customers prefer it. There are no accidents. Every decision your company makes has a reason behind it. You could say:
   - *"Your point is well taken. Our reasoning behind doing it this way is _____. This way we can offer _____."*
   - *"We considered doing it the way you described, but here's why we did it this way instead."*
   - *"A lot of folks told us they prefer it this way because _____."*

Your goal is not to argue with customers, but to introduce them to another viewpoint. Let them see the homes from your perspective, and from the perspective of those who have already purchased. This way you can at least give them a reason – give them permission – to accept the objection if they like everything else about the home better than the other available alternatives.

2. *Explain how they can benefit from tradeoffs.* Explain the benefits they will receive because of the item to which they are objecting. For example, show how you have been able to offer the largest family room in your price range by taking space out of the seldom-used living room. Let them see how you have thought through the entire situation to offer the best of what is most important.

Now let's look at a few other examples of how to use the principles we have discussed so far.

Small Home Sites

Let's say you have a customer who was hoping for a larger home site than you can offer. First you want to find out how important the larger home site really is. You can ask it just like that: *"Is the larger home site a must, or is it just something you were hoping for? Do you have a particular use for the extra square footage, or do you just want as much space as possible?"* It's a sincere question. If the larger site is an absolute necessity, then it's a condition. But if they say they just want more space, you can start out by validating their request. *"That's certainly a reasonable thing to want, especially for this price, but if you don't absolutely need it, here's another idea to consider in terms of getting the best home for your money. For the last forty years, the trend toward smaller home sites has been mostly consumer-driven. Many people who start out wanting a larger site wind up changing their minds. And many people who chose a larger site for their previous home would choose a smaller one if they had it to do over. The reason is that a smaller site allows you to get more home in a better location with less maintenance for less money."* It's a simple and obvious principle, but for many customers it takes awhile for the full impact of it to sink in. They have to visit several places with different lot sizes to realize the sacrifices they must make in order to get a larger lot.

You're not debating whether a large lot is better than a small lot. You are broadening their knowledge to help them make the best decision for their total quality of life by explaining why more people choose small lots over large lots, and that builders have adapted to this consumer preference in order to provide a better total package for the money. If they are open to a new way of thinking, then you are closer to gaining a buying decision than you were before they raised the objection. You could put icing on the cake with a trial close: *"Is that idea something that could work for you?"*

Homes That Back to a Road

Before getting too deep into resolving a road objection with your customer, find out if a sale is really hanging in the balance. It's so easy to say, "I don't want to back up to a road," that the customer may be avoiding other issues that are just as important to their buying decision. You might want to settle that question first by asking, *"Other than the road, how do you like everything else?"* If they really would buy your home if it weren't on a road, and you don't have

The Basics and the Magic

anything available in their time frame or price range that's not on the road, then proceed with your explanation.

Start out by asking, *"How do you feel about the road?" ("What is it about the road that concerns you?")* Let them talk it through. See what it is that is causing the anxiety, and how much anxiety is there. If they are so afraid of the safety issue because of their children or pets that they can't even consider the site, then the objection has reached the level of a condition. But they may merely be responding in a spirit of, "Backing up to a road was never on our wish list. Tell us why it should be." If that is the case, then you can begin with your explanation:

"We have had homes backing up to a road and homes backing up to other homes available at the same time, and many of our buyers have opted for the homes on the road as their first choice. One reason is that the road offers a greater feeling of space, because it's more open than backing up to another home."

People are sometimes concerned about the noise and lack of privacy that a road could produce. Naturally, if there is a privacy fence at the back of the lot, then the privacy issue goes away, and maybe even the noise issue as well. But if there is no fence you could say:

"When people drive by, they have to keep their eyes on the road. They can't pay attention to you the way people living behind you can. A lot of folks who back up to a road feel that their situation is actually more private than backing up to another home.

"As for the sound, there has been a lot of research on this topic that explains why builders keep building homes backing

to roads, and why buyers keep buying them. When people who live in homes backing to this kind of road are asked what it's like, one answer comes up again and again. People say they stopped noticing the sound after a short time. It just became a part of their lives that never bothered them again, because it is not a disruptive sound. But I want to make sure it's something you're comfortable with."

It may seem as though this last sentence is going too far by creating unnecessary risk in the decision, and you can certainly leave it off. But remember that the risk is already there. It's better to confront it with the customer on your terms than to ask the customer to confront it by themselves later, or by asking someone else for advice. In our example here, you are "giving them permission" to buy a home backing to a road if they feel okay about it themselves. You are showing sensitivity for their concerns, but also using third-party testimonials for reassurance. It's a variation of the old "feel, felt, found" theme.

However, some people are simply not capable of buying a home backing to a road. You know that going in. Don't assume it, but be aware of it. Your goal is not to convince everyone that a road is the greatest feature in the world. It is to give them a way to accept the road if they like everything else about your package better than any other alternative they are considering. You want to show compassion, to be the kind of salesperson from whom they want to buy. You are not afraid to lose a sale. You want what's best for the customer, but you are also confident selling homes backing to a road, because hundreds of thousands of people in the United States are happy living in them. You offer your own confidence in the situation along with your reassurance.

A Small Secondary Bedroom

If they express concern that a child's bedroom is too small, begin by asking, *"Do you have an idea of how large you want the room to be?"* Find out how advanced their thought process is. Often, people's first response to a secondary bedroom is that it is small, especially in an affordably priced home. But the issue is not how small the room looks or feels, it is whether the room will adequately fulfill its function, and your builder has already thought through that issue.

Begin by making sure you are the customer's ally in shared purpose. Together you are committed to the mission of improving their lives.

Make sure the issue is important: *"Do you like everything else about the home?"* If they say yes: *"Then let's see if we can figure out a way for this bedroom to meet your child's needs. Remember that kids don't think about the size of a bedroom the same way adults do, and it's not just because they're smaller. We know they're going to get bigger. Kids have a different concept of bedroom size than adults do. Adults are more concerned with how much space is between things. Kids are more concerned about owning the room, and making sure their stuff fits. With kids the room is more about identity than space. This room was designed to hold a double bed, a desk and a dresser, which is pretty good for a secondary bedroom in this price range. But what about your child (use a name if possible)? Will her things fit?"*

Here you are showing personal interest in the child's well-being, but you are also explaining that a sensible thought process went into the distribution of bedroom space. You provide extra space in the master bedroom because of the way adults think about space. Then you provide the right amount of space to meet the child's needs without wasting money on space that will not make a difference in the child's enjoyment of the room.

Then close on the upstairs: *"So does the upstairs work for you?"*

Unless specific furniture or some other need rules out your bedrooms (a condition), customers should be willing to accept smaller secondary bedrooms if:

- They understand your thought process and the purpose of your design.
- They see a corresponding benefit (larger master bedroom for the money).
- They understand that your secondary bedrooms are competitive for your price range.
- They see that you are helping them with their decision with their well-being in mind.
- They like the home enough to own it otherwise.

Keep Customers Focused On the Total Package

In response to objections, we have suggested occasionally asking a customer, *"Other than that, how do you like the rest of the home?"* The point we are making is that the customer must sometimes be reminded that the decision they are making is which *total home* is best for them. As we said earlier, customers will make compromises in any home they buy. If a customer gets too fixated on an objection which you have done all you can to help them resolve, then you need to help them get past it so they can see the bigger picture. But you have to do it respectfully and compassionately. For example:

- *"Even with that one item, is there anything else you've seen you like as well as this?"*
- *"Do you feel you'd be happier here or where you live now?"*
- *"I wish I could give you everything, but I can't, but then neither can anyone else. What I do want to provide for you is the best overall home for the money. How are we doing there?"*

Try to get their focus back to the total balance of features – the total package of what you offer versus the total package of other homes available, including their current home. Customers want the best of everything they have seen combined into one home for the lowest price, but they won't find that anywhere. Your position of strength will never come from satisfying every desire, but from offering them the best total package for the money. It is hard for customers to stay focused on the total package. They need your help.

Handling Value Objections

As with every other part of selling, success in handling value objections hinges largely on attitude. You must not allow yourself to feel vulnerable when a customer tells you your price should be lower. That's what customers are supposed to say. They think they're testing the water. Perhaps they can't afford your home, but that's not a value objection, that's an unqualified customer.

Customers do *not* have the position of strength regarding value. Remember this vital principle: Customers only have the position of strength if they don't want your home, but then position of strength doesn't matter. **Once the customer wants your home, you have the position of strength.** Why? Because no one else can sell them your home, but you can sell your home to someone else.

Think of value objections as one more situation in which customers are "asking your permission" to pay what your home is worth. Perhaps they've seen another home that costs less, or perhaps your price is higher than they had originally planned to pay. So they need permission in order to pay more. They need for someone to tell them there really is a valid reason to pay more, and it really is okay to pay more as long as they can afford it.

With this attitude in mind, let's see how to handle the most frequent value objections customers raise.

"Your Homes Are Priced Too High."

Every builder defines value in a slightly different way. Customers don't understand the concept of value in our industry, so educating them on your company's definition of value is essential to your success in a challenging or competitive market. If you offer the least expensive homes in your market, then your value message is fairly simple. But if your homes are not the least expensive, then you will need to sell the value of your total package. You will need to help them understand the ways in which you offer more home for the money – a better total combination of features.

Suppose a customer says to you, "The builder down the street offers a lower price than you do." You can answer by saying,

- *"Yes, I know they do. We've never been the cheapest home in the market. That's not our goal, and it's not what we're known for. When people choose us, it's because they feel we offer a better total value. Our goal is always to offer the best home for the money, which is a lot different than offering the lowest price. When I say 'best home for the money,' what I mean is _____."* This is where you would explain your unique value benefits – your definition of value. Emphasize any features or policies that set you apart from the competition. You want to show your customers that your company is committed to the concept of value, and that you personally believe in their concept. Here's a slightly different way of saying it:
- *"We're not the cheapest in the market. When you spend more money to build and service a home, you can't be the low-cost producer. No one ever bought a _____ (name of your company) home because it was cheaper. People buy a _____ home because they believe it's the best total home for the money, including square footage, features, architecture, construction standards, service program, location and customer satisfaction."* (Also include home sites and amenities if they are a superior feature.)

"I Want Your Home For Their Price."

This topic overlaps with the last one. However, the emphasis here is on the customer who is simply saying, "Match their price, and you've got yourself a deal." This attitude shows how many customers truly don't get it when it comes to comparing the prices of homes. They're accustomed to comparing the prices of cars, where it's the same car with the same features produced by the same manufacturer with the same MSRP. Deals are easy to compare, so customers can say, "Match their price, and you've got yourself a deal." Consider addressing their challenge this way:

- *"I would love to be able to sell you my home for their price, but I can't. Then again, neither can they. Let me ask you this: if both homes were the same price, which would you choose?"* If the customer says they would choose the competitor's, what are they doing back at your community? However, if they say they would choose yours, you can ask why, and then respond to their answer by saying, *"That's why we're more. It costs us more to provide that."* The benefit of this approach is that it allows your customers to put into their own words why they think your homes are better. Instead of selling them on your value, you are getting them to sell you. One more way of asking the same question is:
- *"Deal aside, which home do you like better?...Why?*

Remind your customers that you are not asking them to change the way they think about value. You're asking them to use the way they already think one more time. People are already willing to spend $100 a month more to get a better car, drink bottled water or get their coffee at a coffee shop. And none of those products offer any investment value or tax deduction. You can get a lot more home for $100 a month, especially after taxes.

"They're Giving a Bigger Discount."

Here the customer is not fixated so much on getting the lowest price or even the best value. Instead, they've gotten it into their heads (possibly using cars as their frame of reference) that getting the best deal or the best value means getting the biggest discount. If someone else is giving a bigger discount (or more incentives) than you are, then it means they're giving a better deal. Here are a few suggestions for getting these customers on to the right track:

- "You can't compare the size of discounts (or price reductions) alone because there are too many other factors."
- "Remember that you can't compare deals in real estate the same way you can in other fields. There are too many variables, and every builder focuses on whichever variable they think is most important."
- "I know it's confusing to go from one place to another and have everyone present you with a different pricing strategy. Just remember, that's what discounting is – a pricing strategy. They charge a high enough price that they can give a bigger discount. A discount is not the same as a deal, and it's not the same as value. I can't give you the lowest price in the market, or the biggest discount. What I can give you is the best home for the money."
- "Everyone in our industry sells a home for as much as they possibly can. They just approach it in different ways. But remember, if someone is giving you $20,000 off the price, they're only doing it because they know if they offered $19,000 off they couldn't sell the home. There's a saying in our industry that the best deal is often on the worst home."

- *"Why do you think they have to offer such big discounts?"*
- *"With them offering such a great deal, why haven't you bought there already?"*
- *"I appreciate the fact that you want the best deal possible. We want to be the ones to give you the best deal and earn your business. Let me ask you this: How will you know when you get the best deal?"*

Are They Worth Fighting For?

When customers keep hammering you about your price, can they even afford your home? Before wasting too much time or energy trying to sell your value to someone who keeps hounding you for a lower price, make sure they're not just wishing they could own a home that they can't possibly afford. Unfortunately, some people have a hard time admitting they can't afford something. Sometimes they're even angry about it, so they try to punish you for charging too much. To get to the truth, ask them:

- *"If you take the deal and the market out of the equation, is this a price you feel you can afford?"* This may lead into a conversation about qualifying.

Get Their Focus Back On To the Home

If they become so fixated on getting a lower price or a better deal that they are no longer focusing on the home, you need to help them regain their balance and see the bigger picture. This challenge can seem especially daunting in a buyer's market, where customers believe they are holding all the cards. Consider this approach, especially if tough market conditions are in play:

- *"There is one thing we always see during slower housing markets where getting a great deal takes center stage. The more a buyer focuses on the deal when they buy, the more likely they are to want to cancel their contract later. That's because they didn't fulfill their original mission, which was to get a home they really wanted. The real victory in a buyer's market is not to get the best deal, because there's no way to know which deal is best. Even appraisers can't figure that one out. The real victory is to get the home you want and get a great price on it, which you will. In this market all the prices are great, regardless of which discounting strategy the builder is using."*

Here you are reestablishing your role as counselor and leader, and also your sense of joint purpose with your customers in the quest of improving their lives, which is what your relationship is supposed to be about. You want to get your customers back into the frame of mind where together you can focus on the important questions: *"Would you be happy here?...Would you be happier here than where you live now?...Would you be happier here than anyplace else you've seen?...Then that's the important thing. Now we just have to put our heads together and figure out a way to get you where you want to go."*

Conclusion

Think of objections as friends, not enemies – as opportunities to make sales, not lose them. Objections are a healthy and necessary part of a customer's decision process. Raising objections and then resolving them is part of the system of checks and balances that helps customers make decisions with greater confidence – decisions they won't regret later.

Objections provide opportunities to:

- Better understand the needs of your customers
- Connect with them through a sense of shared purpose
- Provide leadership to them
- Help them to better understand the benefits you provide, as well as the reasoning behind the approach you take and the decisions you make
- Help them to rethink and evolve their needs

Recognize the differences between objections and conditions. Don't get frustrated with yourself or your product when you lose sales over conditions. These are not really lost sales anyway. They were never meant to be sales, because people with insurmountable conditions are not your market.

As in other dimensions of selling, preparation will provide you an enormous advantage in handling objections.

For this chapter's follow through exercise, write down the top ten objections you anticipate or currently face at your community. We're talking about any kind of objection – product, price, home sites, location, community, or advantages your competition has over you. What are the top ten? Prepare a strategy for handling each of them, including the following issues to whatever extent they apply:

- Is the objection really an objection, or is it a condition?
- How important is the objection? Will it really affect the outcome of their buying decision?

- What can you do, through questions or suggestions, to help them think their concern all the way through, verbalizing their thoughts as they go so that you both understand them?
- How will you establish yourself as the leader and counselor in the relationship?
- How can you help them to rethink and evolve their needs by:
  1. Explaining why you chose the approach you did
  2. Explaining how they can benefit from favorable tradeoffs

Remember that you will ultimately have to get their focus back on to those things about your home they like the most – the things that will enable them to fulfill their original mission of improving their lives.

When customers raise objections, consider that they may be "asking for permission" to accept the objection as long as they are getting the best home for themselves overall – the one that will most improve their lives for a price they can afford. This is especially crucial for objections concerning price or value.

To successfully handle value objections you must know your surrounding market well enough to be able to express the ways in which you offer a better value than your competition. You must also know their advantages so that you can counter them effectively and still believe that your homes adhere to a higher definition of value. Every builder defines value in a slightly different way. Be sure you understand your company's definition of value at your community, and the ways in which you offer a better value than anyone else.

Use the principles and examples from the final section of this chapter – "Handling Value Objections" – to prepare answers for challenges you anticipate involving price, value or discounts. With value objections you should practice your approach with someone else to see if it sounds convincing to them as well as to you.

The Basics and the Magic

Chapter 6

CLOSING

Closing is magical, but it's not mysterious. When you ask customers to make a decision that will improve their lives and they say yes, magic is in the air. These customers are about to begin an exciting, life-changing adventure, and you are the one who helped them chart their course. You guided them where they wanted to go. You profoundly influenced their lives in a wonderful way. You did it by understanding them, connecting with them, enlightening them, leading them, and being there for them as someone they could trust and lean on.

Closing is the most rewarding part of the sale – not just financially, but also in the sense of accomplishment. Yet with all of its wonder and significance and rewards, closing is also the easiest and most natural part of the sale. You close simply because you've done everything else. You've rounded every other base on the diamond, and there's only one left. You ask for the sale because you've gotten there. So magical, and yet so simple. So awesome, and yet so obvious.

We are talking about closing as though it is a single moment in time – that magical moment when you ask for the sale. In one sense it is. There is a *closing moment* when you bring to a conclusion everything that has gone before. You close your customers because so often they are unable to close themselves. They need for you to take them by the hand and lead them on to one last bridge over one last canyon. Without you to show them the way, they will fall in – swallowed up by the magnitude of the decision.

But closing is more than just a defining moment at the end of the sale. It is also an entire process – a sequence of decisions – through which you guide customers by knowing the basics of closing and applying them consistently. *Closing is a series of decisions by the customer that results from a series of initiatives by you.*

What makes a good closer? Is it a higher level of skill? Partly. Is it developing a higher level of trust with your customers? Partly. Is it the five special demeanors we have emphasized throughout this book? Absolutely. When it comes time to bring the sale home, make sure your customers see once again the elements in you that are such an important part of their buying experience: confidence, enthusiasm, joy, purpose and relaxation. Closing includes all of these attributes, but it is more. **Closing is a total way of thinking.**

How a Great Closer Thinks

Great closing involves the magic of selling, and the magic does not come from techniques alone. Throughout this book we have seen how the magic of selling comes from a combination of attitude, temperament and demeanor. The same applies to the magic of closing. If you start out with the right mindset, then the right behavior, techniques and timing will follow naturally. So let's look first at a strong mindset that empowers a strong closer, and then we'll look at style.

We can gain insight into how great closers think – what makes them tick – by revisiting some of the topics from our first two chapters. Let's begin by reviewing those magic sources that relate directly to closing.

Focus On Resolution Throughout the Sale

Great closers are resolution-oriented by nature. At their central core they feel an unconditional commitment to achieving resolution. They do not wait for the final close to pursue resolution, but focus on resolving the customer's questions, needs, thoughts and concerns every step of the way. They realize that the questions a salesperson asks throughout the sale, and the decisions that result from these questions, provide the framework of the closing process.

The temperament of strong closers is purposeful, so they connect with customers on the level of shared purpose – joining forces with them as an ally in their mission to improve their lives through a decision process. **The strongest connection you can establish with your customers is the connection of shared purpose.** Your desire for resolution makes you more interested in who they are, what they want, and what they are thinking each step of the way. This interest helps you connect with them on a deeper level.

A purposeful temperament also makes strong closers more motivated, more energized, and more unstoppable.

Provide Leadership

Great closers assume a leadership role in their relationships with customers. They assume this role easily and confidently because they realize it's what a serious customer wants and expects of an expert. Whenever we are trying to find our way in strange and frightening territory, we want a guide we can count on. We want the leadership of an expert. So you don't merely engage customers, you lead them. You don't just monitor their decision process, you lead it. This helps give customers the confidence they need to keep moving forward. They know they're in good hands. They know they have found the right salesperson from whom to buy.

Just as customers expect you to lead, they also expect you to close. That's one of the things that make closing so easy. As with demonstration and other services of selling, there's no reason to over think whether customers want to be closed. They expect it, and they are surprised when it doesn't happen.

Sell As Though Customers Will Buy

Assume that every customer who walks in your door will buy – and treat them as though they will buy – until they prove to you that they won't. If they are serious about improving their lives with a new home, they will appreciate that you take them seriously. **Great closers see opportunities where other salespeople don't.**

When you sell as though customers will buy, you engage and connect with them at a deeper level. You become more interested in them, and they see it. You sell with more energy and purpose. You provide a better experience. You ask more questions to learn their needs, you provide more solutions to help them meet their needs, and you give them more insight to help them rethink their needs – all of which help create a decision-making rhythm.

Make Customers Feel Wanted

We have talked about making customers see that you want their business more than anyone else does. You make them feel more wanted by being more interested in them, caring more about them, and trying harder to earn their business. One of the best ways to make customers feel wanted is by asking them to buy your home – to be your customer – to become a member of your community.

In Chapter Four we discussed the focus group study in which buyers expressed disappointment that most salespeople did not want to demonstrate, ask for the sale, or follow up. This translated into a perception of professional negligence, and also of leaving customers feeling unwanted.

If a qualified customer has picked a favorite home and site, why would a salesperson not ask that customer to buy the home? Does the salesperson not want their business? Even if the customer originally said, "I'll be making a decision in about a year," that was then and this is now.

The same applies to a customer who is sticking with the process but not acting as excited as you would like. Some people adopt a serious demeanor when making a serious decision. Or maybe they're just not expressive by nature. Even if you think their answer might be no, you ask them to buy in order to make them feel wanted. As we said above, customers expect a salesperson to ask them to buy, and if he doesn't ask something is wrong.

Don't Stop the Sale

One source of magic in selling is a *momentum mentality*. Great closers cherish momentum from the minute a customer walks in their door. Whatever stage of the sale they're in, they always want to go one stage farther. They want to get the customer to do one more thing. They want to get to the next base on the diamond.

But is it a stretch to call this closing? Not at all, because closing is not just a moment in time, but a total way of thinking. A momentum mentality – the desire to keep the sale moving forward – is driven by a resolution-oriented temperament, a leadership mentality, an attitude that every customer will buy until they prove they won't, and a desire to make customers feel more wanted than anyone else does.

Momentum is a mindset – part of a closer's total way of thinking. A momentum mentality is simple: **Only the customer can stop the sale, never the salesperson.** A great closer does not over think the subtleties of a customer's body language, eye contact or voice tone. They keep it simple by thinking: **"If the customer is still here, I'll take that as a yes."**

Take the Right Approach to Urgency

We had a deliberate reason for addressing urgency early in this book – we presented it before discussing the selling process instead of waiting until this chapter on closing. If we rely too much upon urgency as a closing tool, we wind up feeling helpless when we're not able to create it. Creating urgency through a single circumstance or strategy should be considered a relatively small part of selling. Instead, **think of urgency as something that grows along with the customer's interest in your home.**

Closing

While there are times we can create urgency instantly at the end to close a sale, we should think of these sales as a gift, not as a way to make a living. Instead, review the following concepts regarding urgency that we discussed in Chapter Two.

1. Give urgency time to develop. Unless there is some circumstance driving a customer's need to act quickly, do not expect urgency to begin until they want your home. Then help the urgency to develop through the seven steps we listed in Chapter Two.
2. Understand that urgency grows more often from confidence than from fear. Continue to nurture the customer's confidence that they are doing the right thing through the steps suggested in Chapter Two.

Once you accept this attitude as the best for seeing the big picture of urgency, there will still be times when you can create immediate urgency for a customer to buy your home today. Examples would be:

- The customer needs to move quickly because of his particular situation.
- You are offering a limited-time incentive.
- You have a limited supply of what the customer wants, and other customers will also want it in the near future.
- You have one particular home or lot that a customer doesn't want to lose.
- You have an imminent price increase.

Of course you want to take advantage of these opportunities whenever they present themselves. Here are a few other ideas for creating the kind of urgency that closes a sale.

Sell One of a Kind

You have previously created a list of reasons why every home site you have (or every unit, in the case of condominiums) is unique. No matter how similar your sites may be, there will be one that is a customer's favorite, even if the advantage is small. Whichever one is their favorite could be the next customer's favorite as well.

If a customer is waffling and is not ready to buy that day, you can say, *"I certainly understand not wanting to move too fast. You don't want to make a decision you'll regret. While you're here, as long as you've picked out a favorite, which one is your second choice?"* The customer might wonder why you've asked such a question. You can explain, *"The reasons you picked that home site make good sense. Usually, when we have one site that has an advantage over the others, it's the next one to sell. If you come back and someone else felt the same way you do, we'll have to go with Plan B."* Now they will have to deal with the issue of whether the biggest investment of their lives is going to wind up being the leftovers from someone else who was more decisive.

As their partner in their mission, you don't have to say, "If you don't buy it someone else will." Instead, you can take a more benevolent approach: *"If this is the home for you, I want to be sure you're the one who gets it."*

Anecdotes Are Powerful

Anecdotes are a powerful selling tool in any stage of the sale. Of course they must be sensitive and the timing must be right. When creating urgency through fear of loss, consider whether you have any anecdotes that might be helpful for the customer who is on the fence but seems to want a push. Notice we say "want" a push instead of "need" a push, because that's the way it is with many customers, especially those who come back multiple times. Imagine they are saying, "I keep coming back because I want a bigger push." For these customers consider telling anecdotes of others who have hesitated and lost, including yourself. The fact is that in real estate, with rare exceptions such as overheated, over-inflated markets, people who make the decision to buy are almost always glad they did, while people who decide to wait usually regret it.

You could say, *"One of the worst things that happens in my line of work is when customers want to buy but don't act on it, and then wind up disappointed. Either the financial terms aren't as good, or something happens on their end that makes it tougher to move. Sometimes they even take it out on me for not warning them."*

Another approach would be to tell about someone who did act, even when they were scared, and wound up being glad they did.

Don't Try to Create Urgency Too Soon

Before the days of repeating rifles, the expression, "Don't fire until you see the whites in their eyes," meant, "Don't shoot before the target is in range. You'll waste your shot, and then you won't have another chance." In creating urgency, don't use your ammunition until the customer wants your home. If you hit customers too hard, too soon with messages such as, "You'd better act now because they're going fast," or, "Let me tell you about our incentives," you'll be firing your shots before the target is in range. By the time the target moves into range (the customer decides they want your home), your gun will be empty. It is okay to convey such information as a way of demonstrating value or showing that exciting things are happening at your community. Just don't expect this kind of information to create urgency until the customer has something to feel urgent about. Remember that most customers can't focus on urgency or time frame until after they decide on the home they want.

Closing Creates an Urgency All Its Own

There will be times when the first urgency a customer feels is awakened by your invitation to buy. Before that moment they felt no urgency because the decision to buy was never on the table. They went from one community to the next where the salesperson said, "Call me if you have any questions," so buying was never part of their reality. For many customers, buying a home remains a fantasy until someone asks them to do it. The closing question awakens them from their dream and confronts them with the truth of their intentions. It forces them to face the question, "Now that I have the opportunity to improve my life, what will it mean if I say no? Am I really serious about improving my life, or is this all just a hopeless fantasy?" They may surprise you by deciding that they want to go ahead now that they have worked through this internal confrontation, or they may need to wrestle with it a little more at home. This moment of truth can sometimes be the greatest motivator of all. By asking for the sale you have brought the decision to the forefront of their consciousness, where it belongs.

Now that we have taken a look inside the mind of a great closer, let's turn those thoughts into action.

How Closing Develops

When does closing begin? It begins with your first questions that require a statement of purpose for an answer, such as:

- *"Are you thinking of making a move?"*
- *"What is it that's gotten you thinking about moving?"*
- *"Have you set any sort of timetable yet?"*
- *"Have you decided on a price or payment that you don't want to go above?"*

Any question that relates to any aspect of the customer's purpose or plan is a preliminary closing question, because it relates to a buying decision, however trivial that decision may seem. The purpose of a preliminary closing question is not, of course, to make a sale, but rather to elicit a decision, and eventually to establish a *decision-making rhythm*.

Beware of Pretender Syndrome

In Chapter Five we suggested observing your customers' behavior patterns regarding decisions. Now let's dig a little deeper into that idea.

The willingness to make decisions is a customer's most reliable buying signal. If a customer continually deflects decisions, it could be a sign of "pretender syndrome." Let the selling process evolve as far as possible before reaching a conclusion, since some customers are not motivated to make decisions until they have decided they are truly interested in buying your home. Nevertheless, if the pattern of deflecting decisions continues, you may have to address their intentions with a question such as, *"How do you feel about the whole idea of making a move?"*

Here are a few of the ways that customers may reveal a pattern of deflecting decisions:

- They continue to raise one objection after another. The objections are frequently all over the place – that is to say, they have nothing to do with each other – and are frequently objections the customer does not believe you can resolve.
- They make requests they do not believe you can fulfill. One of the symptoms of pretender syndrome is when a customer says, in one way or another, "If you can do for me what I already know you can't do for me, I'll buy your home."
- They want a home that is not available – for example, a future section. This is not to say that they will never buy that future home, but we have all experienced the buyer who nags and nags us about a home that is not yet released, but when we release it for them they find a new excuse not to buy.
- When confronted with decisions, they repeatedly make a joke or change the subject.

If you suspect pretender syndrome, it doesn't mean you should give your customer the brushoff, but it does mean you need to get a handle on how they feel about the whole idea of moving. You may also want to review:

- Why they are looking for a home
- How much discontent they feel with their current situation
- How they really feel about your homes
- How comfortable they are with the price of the home you are discussing

Keep It Simple

Closing is the simplest, most obvious behavior in the world. You keep asking questions because you are interested in what your customers think, and how they feel about what they are seeing and hearing. **Sell to a customer as though you are selling to a friend.** If a friend comes to you because they want to improve their lives with a better home, you want them to experience your homes in the richest, most complete way possible. You want to show more interest in them, treat them better, and help them more than anyone else they visit. And you want to know how you're doing in helping them fulfill their mission. You're not only interested, you're also focused on achieving resolution and completing the mission. You want to sell them a home because they came to you wanting to buy one.

In order to stay on track, you would ask questions as you go in order to get the best possible feedback. If they get stuck, you would provide opinions of your own *("Would you like to know what I think?")* to help them break their logjam.

Ask Questions to Sustain Momentum

In Chapter Four on demonstrating homes and sites, we discussed a variety of questions to get the kind of feedback that keeps you moving forward, and to establish the customer's decision-making rhythm. By the end of the site visit we were transitioning into questions that set up the close. Let's pick up where we left off there. Here are some examples of questions that lead you toward the final close – making that climactic moment easier, more natural and more successful.

- *"Do you feel as though you're making some progress?"*

- "Is this (Have you found) what you were looking (hoping) for?"
- "From what you've seen so far, what do you think?"
- "Does this look (feel) like it's coming together for you?" ("What do you think? Are the pieces fitting together?")
- "Do you feel like there are any loose ends?"
- "When you first came in, you mentioned that you were looking for _____. How does this compare with what you were hoping for?"
- "From what you told me earlier, it looks like we've found what you were looking (hoping) for." Just make this statement and then wait for the customer to respond.
- "How is all this looking to you?" ("Is this looking pretty good to you?")
- "How does all this feel to you?" ("Do you have a good feeling about all this?") ("I have a really good feeling about this. How about you?")
- "I get the feeling you really like (want) this home. Is that true?"
- "Does this look like something you'd be happy with?"
- "How do you feel about the idea of living here?" ("Do you think you'd enjoy living here?") ("Do you think you'd be happy here?") ("Can you see yourself living here some day?")
- "Are we a possibility for you?"
- "Does this look like the one?"
- "Do you think we might get the chance to have you as a customer (neighbor)?"
- "Do you think we might fit into your future plans?"
- "What is your game plan at this point?" ("What's your next step?")

Wrap It Up in a Bow

It is now time to bring the sale home, and once again the basics and the magic come together. For the basics, it's knowing how and when to close with the right skills and techniques. For the magic, it's making sure the close is a great moment in which your customers now share your confidence, enthusiasm, joy, relaxation and purpose as they finalize the decision that completes their quest. Let's see how it happens.

You create closing opportunities by hitting triples. Once customers have picked a favorite home and site, and you have determined that they have the ability to buy your home, you've *earned the right to close*, and you don't want to let them leave your community without asking for the sale.

There will be times when customers close themselves with a remark such as, "We love this home. What's the next step?" But most of the time you will have to initiate the closing moment. You want to have several approaches with which you feel comfortable, so that when the moment comes you can get through it easily, confidently and seamlessly. You don't want any awkward pauses, just full steam ahead. Asking for the sale is the obvious thing to do.

If you are at the site, you could ask for the sale as simply as this: *"Would you like to have this home?"* (or, *"Do you like this home?...*If they say yes, *"Would you like to have it?"*)

If you sense that the customer is feeling skittish, and a less direct approach would be more effective, you could say: *"When folks decide they want to take a home off the market, the way it works is…"* You explain the process for buying a home, and then follow through with a closing question such as, *"What do you think?"* or, *"Are you ready to do that?"* or, *"Would you like to take this home off the market?"*

Following is a menu of closes for different situations and also for different personality types – yours as well as the customers'. The more comfortable you are with your closing style, the more comfortable they will be. Choose several from among the following list (or from your own experience) so you can adapt to whether your customers are chomping at the bit to get on with it, or perhaps feel more reluctant, or still seem to be chasing a few loose ends around in their mind.

They don't have to be 100% certain in order for you to ask for the sale. Sometimes they will never resolve their loose ends and become certain until a closing question takes them there. The closing question is frequently the vehicle that elevates their thought process to the level where they can resolve the decision. Even when a close brings a negative response, it may still be the catalyst that gets them closer to their ultimate decision to buy. While their answer may be "no" today, your closing question has still gotten them closer to a "yes" in the near future.

We are providing this assortment of closes as a simple list, because the situation for which each question is most appropriate will be self-evident.

- *"Would you like to go ahead and take this home off the market?"* (*"Would you like me to go ahead and take this home off the market for you?"*)
- *"Would you like to have this home?"*
- *"Is this the one for you?"* (*"Have you found the one for you?"*) (*"Have you found the home that will make you happy?"*) (*"Have you found what you were*

looking for?")
- *"This all looks perfect. Let's go ahead and make it yours."*
- *"It looks like we're all set. Let's go for it."*
- *"Are you ready to go ahead with the next step?"*
- *"Are you ready to put a sold sign on this home?"*
- *"Would you like to see how this looks on paper?"* (*"Would you like to start going over some of the forms?"*) (*"Would you like to go ahead and start the paperwork?"*)
- *"Do you feel ready to take the next step (to go to the next stage)?"*
- *"If you are interested in going ahead with the next step, what we would do is…"* Explain the next step… *"Would you like to do that?"*
- *"Do you feel you want to discuss it a little further, or would you like to move forward?"*
- *"Are there any other issues you need to resolve in order to make a decision you'll feel good about?"*
- *"Is there anything about this home you don't like?"* (*"…that doesn't work for you?"*) (*"…that concerns you?"*) (*"…that you don't feel good about?"*)
- *"On a scale of one to ten, how do you like it?"* This would be for a situation where you feel you need a little more insight into where you stand before you ask the final closing question. If the number they give you is lower than you were hoping: *"What is it that's between us and a ten?"*

It's Not the End When the Customer Says "No"

Your goal for closing is not solely to make a sale that day. It is sometimes simply to advance the customers' decision process and make them feel wanted. Even when your close fails to achieve a sale that day, it still succeeds in maximizing whatever opportunity exists. Asking for the sale is a way to achieve resolution, even if the resolution is that the customer will not buy your home. You will never lose a sale because you ask a customer to buy. They expect you to ask. Asking for the sale helps you learn the truth of their intentions.

When a customer says "no" after you ask them to buy, it is not a rejection. They are simply telling you they are not ready to buy your home at that moment. Even if they say they can never buy your home because it isn't the right home for them, you need to know this so you can devote your energy to other efforts that are more productive.

Just as you have prepared for what comes next at every stage of the sale, you need to prepare what you will do when a customer declines your invitation to buy. You don't want this to be an awkward moment, and you don't want to feel defeated. You have already hit a triple, and a triple is a good hit. But now you want to keep going, just as when handling objections. We discussed that when it's time to ask for the sale, you want to be prepared with what you will say so you can create a seamless transition. The same applies now. When the customer says "no," you want to create a seamless transition to the next stage of the sale.

It is vital that you not lose your sense of purpose during this moment, unless, of course, the customer says they can never buy your home and gives you an ironclad explanation.

Otherwise there is plenty of purpose left. When customers say "no," your next purposes are to:

- Keep them feeling comfortable.
- Continue to make them feel wanted.
- Find out where you stand.
- Uncover the issues behind their reluctance.
- Go as far as you can in resolving those issues.
- Try again to close the sale.
- If the sale is impossible that day, set up the next step.

As with asking for the sale, we will provide a menu of possibilities depending on how they respond to your close. You may need to ask if there are any new issues, or review ones that you have discussed but not resolved, or you may need to learn more about their overall state of mind. If you conclude that they are simply not ready to buy, then your best course of action is to see if they can express their future intentions. The following questions address this variety of possibilities.

- *"Do you have any concerns we haven't addressed?" ("Is there anything you're not completely comfortable with?")*
- *"I know there are a lot of things about this home you like."* Review those things. *"Is there anything you don't like?" ("Are there any concerns we didn't address?")*
- *"I get the feeling you really like this home. Is that true?"* Wait for their answer. *"Is there anything that doesn't work for you?" ("Is there anything holding you back?")*
- *"I've really enjoyed spending this time with you, and I hope we're able to have you as a customer (neighbor)*

(part of our community) at some point. Are there any concerns I can help you with?" *("Is there anything about this home that you're still not quite comfortable with?")*

- *"I know you're not ready to make a final decision today. What is your game plan at this point? (What will be your next step?)"*
- Here's one we've discussed previously, but it deserves another look: *"I can certainly understand not wanting to move too fast. You don't want to make a decision you'll regret. While you're here, as long as you've picked out your favorite, which one is your second choice?"*
- *"Would you be happy here?"* *("How do you feel about the idea of living here?")*
- If they say they need to look at some other places: *"If you don't see anything else you like as well as this, do you think this is a home you'd be happy with?"*
- *"Will I be seeing you again?"*
- *"I know you're concerned about making the right decision, but how will you know when you've found the right home?"*
- *"We talked about how great it will be when you finally do get a new home, and it seems from what you have said that life really will be a lot better for you here (… that you'll be very happy here)."* Then just wait for them to respond.
- *"By November (or whenever the home is scheduled for completion), would you rather be living here or in the place where you live now?"*
- *"On a scale of one to ten, with ten meaning you'd buy the home, how much do you like it?"* If they answer

five or higher: *"What is it that's standing between you and a ten?"*

Keep the conversation going as long as the customer is willing to engage. Assume that this is the exactly the conversation they need (and perhaps even want) in order to achieve the breakthrough that will get them where they were trying to go when they began their search.

This is especially true for the buyer who has been back several times, and continues to be on the fence. Assume that the reason they keep coming back is they want a push. They may even want you to tell them what to do. It's worth a try, and you won't be any worse off if it doesn't work. A few examples would be:

- *"Would you like to know what I think?"*
- *"Here's what I would do if I were in your shoes..."*
- *"From everything you've told me, what I would suggest is..."*
- *"You need to do this."*
- *"If this is the home for you, you (we) need to make sure you're the one who gets it."*
- *"Let me just ask you the obvious question: Do you think you'd be happy here?...Is there anything you don't think you'd be happy with?...You seem like you want to go ahead and get this over with so you can get on with your life."*

Having said all of this, there will be times when you won't have to use any of it. You may have done such a great job every step of the way that when you get to the close it's a no-brainer.

- *"Let's go for it."*

- *"Let's get this done."*
- *"Let's get this wrapped up."*
- *"Are you all set?"*
- *"Are you ready to write this up?"*

You may even present your closing line as a joke *("Would you like me to ring this up for you?")*, or the customer may beat you to the punch *("We're ready. What's the next step?")*. But you always want to have an arsenal of techniques you can draw upon when you need them. Knowing that you have these tools for the closing moment will help you sell with greater confidence in the stages of the sale that lead up to the close, making the closing moment easier still.

Once you've taken the sale as far as you can for the day, the next step is to pave the way for follow up. Following up is one more way to make your customers feel wanted, and one more competitive advantage over other salespeople who are less diligent in this aspect of selling. While follow up is beyond the scope of this book which focuses on the face-to-face part of selling, we want to leave you with this thought for continuing the sale after the visit is completed: As with every other stage of the sale, get your customers to look forward to your follow up call with a final comment like this:

- *"It's been a real pleasure getting to know you folks. I appreciate you coming out and spending this time with me, and I hope we get to have you as a customer. In fact, if it's okay with you, I'd love to stay in touch with you to see how your search is coming."* If you would feel more comfortable putting your follow up request in the form of a question, you could ask, *"Is it okay if I keep in touch with you to see how your search is coming?"*

- Assuming they say yes, you can then begin your follow up call by picking up where you left off: *"Hi, this is _____ (your name) with _____ (your company) at _____ (your community). I just wanted to say thanks again for visiting. As I said when you were here, I really enjoyed your visit, so I wanted to give you a follow up call. Now that you've had a few days to reflect back your visit, how are you feeling about it? Do you think we may still be a possibility for you?"* If they say yes, offer any new information that might be helpful. Then move into open-ended questions such as, *"How is your search coming?"*

Conclusion

Throughout this book we have explored not only the basics and magic of selling, but also the joy of it. We're always at our best when we love what we do, and there's a lot to love about selling new homes.

We have explained how to bring the basics of selling together with the magic. In covering the basics, we have discussed a variety of strategies and skills for completing each stage of the sale as productively as possible. The magic is less tangible because it depends largely upon your selling temperament and attitudes. The magic of selling seems more innate than the skills, yet it, too, can be learned, developed and continuously improved. The magic of selling involves five demeanors:

- Confidence

- Enthusiasm
- Joy
- Relaxation
- Purpose

Yet the magic is also much more. To develop your own magic you must combine your selling skills with a commitment to the following ideas:

- A genuine passion for selling
- A desire to connect with customers
- A desire to achieve resolution
- A willingness to assume the leadership role in your relationships with customers
- An attitude of selling to customers as though they will buy
- A desire to make customers feel wanted
- A commitment never to stop the sale
- A wholesome competitive spirit
- A continuous desire to keep improving

If you develop the five demeanors and commit to the ideas listed above, you will improve your ability to:

- Express your market position persuasively
- Keep the sale moving forward with a momentum mentality and an ability to keep your customers wanting to do one more thing
- Create a sense of shared purpose with your customers that helps build trust
- Help your customers to turn partial thoughts into complete ones
- Create urgency throughout the selling process so you don't need contrived circumstances (The

magic of selling is about temperament and style, not "magic bullets.")

The magic of selling also includes the right kind of motivation. As Rich Tiller and Paul Renker explain in their book, *Motivation from the Heart,* the primary source of motivation at its deepest level is belief in yourself and belief in your purpose. The strongest evidence of motivation is the continuous desire to improve.

Throughout this book we have described how the basics and magic enhance each other in every stage of the selling process, from the greeting through the demonstration to the close.

Here are four ways to follow through on what we have discussed about closing.

1. Are there any improvements you can make to earlier stages of the sale that will enhance the quality of your customers' feedback or their decision-making rhythm? Are there any techniques for making your demonstrations more resolution-oriented, so that closing the sale will be easier when the time comes?
2. Decide on a closing style that will always come easily when you have reached the closing stage but are not sure what the customer's answer will be.
3. Decide on a post-closing style for when the customer says "no" – that is to say, a few questions that you can ask with confidence in order to keep the conversation moving forward in a comfortable way.
4. Decide on a way that you will say good-bye to visitors you could not close but for whom you remain hopeful – a way to make them feel wanted and set up your follow up call.

The Basics and the Magic

The basics of selling belong to our profession, but the magic belongs to you. Mastering both brings you a balance of joy and prosperity that few professions offer as richly as new home sales.